D1545501

GOVERNANCE
&
PUBLIC SECURITY

GOVERNANCE
& PUBLIC SECURITY

 Campbell Public Affairs Institute

The PricewaterhouseCoopers Endowment for
The Business of Government

Copyright (c) 2002 Campbell Public Affairs Institute
Maxwell School of Citizenship and Public Affairs, Syracuse University
Syracuse, New York 13244-1090
http://www.campbellinstitute.org
All Rights Reserved

First Edition 2002

Library of Congress Cataloging-in-Publication Data
Available upon request from
Campbell Public Affairs Institute

ISBN 0-9720512-0-1

Printed in Canada

CONTENTS

PREFACE

The papers included in this book were presented at a symposium on Governance and Public Security held at the Maxwell School of Citizenship and Public Affairs on January 18, 2002. The symposium was organized by the Campbell Public Affairs Institute, an interdisciplinary research center within the Maxwell School that promotes research and dialogue on critical issues in governance.

The Institute began organizing this seminar in the weeks following the terror attacks of September 11, 2001. It was clear that those attacks, and the aftershocks felt in subsequent months, had posed profound challenges to governments at all levels and in many different sectors. The events of Fall 2001 revealed dangerous weaknesses in governmental capacities and compelled us to reconsider the wisdom of earlier approaches to the management and organization of critical public services.

The experts who gathered at the Maxwell School in January 2002 — all leaders in their fields — made clear that urgent reforms are needed in many parts of American government. We have published and distributed this collection with the hope that it will provide a useful guide to academics and students interested in contributing to the ongoing debate on the challenge of ensuring homeland security.

The Campbell Public Affairs Institute was established in 1998 as a tribute to Alan K. Campbell, a distinguished academic and public servant. Affectionately known as Scotty, Campbell was a powerful influence on his students and colleagues at the Maxwell School of Citizenship and Public Affairs at Syracuse University during the 1960s and 1970s, first as creator and director of the Metropolitan Studies Program and then as dean of the school from 1969 to 1976. Scotty Campbell was also dedicated to public service, serving as deputy controller of the State of New York, and later as director of the U.S. Office of Personnel Management. He led the legislative effort that resulted in the Civil Service Reform Act of 1978.

The Institute is grateful to the contributors for their commitment to this project during an exceptionally busy time. That the symposium ran so smoothly is largely due to the skill and effort of Bethany Walawender, assistant director of the Institute, and Kelley Coleman, our office coordinator. We would like to thank Alyssa Colonna and Margie Wachtel for their work in preparing manuscripts for publication, and also Mark Howes and the Publications Unit of the Queen's University School of Policy Studies, for graphic design and production work. The Information and Communication Technology program of the Maxwell School did an outstanding job of webcasting the symposium.

We also wish to express our appreciation to our funding partners: the PricewaterhouseCoopers Endowment for the Business of Government, and the Canadian Consultate General, Buffalo. Mark Abramson, executive director of the PricewaterhouseCoopers Endowment, provided invaluable advice and encouragement.

We would appreciate readers' comments on this volume and the work of the Institute. Our Web address is http://www.campbellinstitute.org. Our e-mail address is info@campbellinstitute.org.

Alasdair Roberts
Director
Campbell Public Affairs Institute

REFLECTIONS ON TERRORISM AND PUBLIC MANAGEMENT

William T. Gormley, Jr.

In Richard Adams' (1972) book, *Watership Down*, a community of rabbits has a sudden, disturbing revelation. For some time, they have grown plump on a diet of carrots and lettuce. They have romped happily through the pastures and explored the outer perimeters of their warren. Suddenly, they discover that all is at risk, in the form of lethal human intervention. For the community of rabbits, this mortal threat triggers the animal world's equivalent of a paradigm shift and a decision to seek a safer home.

A paradigm shift does not always flow from a crisis or threat. Even a serious threat may trigger incremental responses, as in Hoover's response to the Great Depression. Alternatively, governments may opt for a series of experimental shots in the dark, as in Roosevelt's response to the same phenomenon. Although we now associate the New Deal with a paradigm shift towards a stronger central government and a stronger presidency, it is worth recalling that the new paradigm became apparent only after the Roosevelt administration's initial and largely successful improvisations. The intellectual rationale for the policy shift emerged along with the new policies and not before them.

A NEW PARADIGM

No one, I think, would claim that a full-blown deductive theory underlies the U.S. government's early response to the tragic and alarming events of September 11. Cabinet secretaries have contradicted themselves and stumbled in their public utterances; shrill rhetoric has waxed and waned; positions have hardened and then softened. Still, a paradigm shift may well be underway, even if the nation's principal policymakers are only dimly aware of it. In this paper, I sketch the broad outlines of that paradigm shift, as I see it. I focus especially on the roles to be played by public agencies at all levels of government, because it is the executive branch in particular that has suddenly found itself in the spotlight, facing high public expectations and deadlines that only our adversaries know for sure.

Trust in Government

The first and arguably most important element of the paradigm shift is growing appreciation for government officials and the growing conviction that the government and not the private sector must solve the new threats to our homeland security. This reverses a long period of decline in the public's confidence in specific political institutions and, more broadly, in government itself. In the wake of September 11, the percentage of Americans who believe the government in Washington can be trusted to do what is right most of the time or just about always increased from 44 percent to 60 percent (Gallup 2001). Confidence in the Congress and the president also improved dramatically. Although longitudinal data are not available for key bureaucracies, approval levels for the U.S. Postal Service and the Centers for Disease Control and Prevention are both quite high.

An early test of whether changing levels of trust in government would have public policy impacts emerged in the debate over whether airport security personnel should be public or private. Despite opposition from Republican members, Congress decided to require all airport security personnel to be public employees, at least in the short run. At the same time, Congress authorized the creation of a new Transportation Security Administration within the Department of Transportation. The federalization of our airport security workforce will add 28,000 employees to the federal bureaucracy, an increase of approximately 1.5 percent. This reverses a steady decline in the number of federal employees during the Clinton years.

The Revival of Planning

The second element of the paradigm shift is growing appreciation for planning as a government function and the growing conviction that we need to be able to anticipate threats and prevent terrorists from carrying out their diabolical plots in the first place. Although planning is hardly a novel concept, it does represent an abrupt departure from the emphasis on accountability that characterized reform efforts from the 1970s through the 1990s. If accountability exemplifies ex post control, planning epitomizes ex ante control. Whereas accountability is backward-looking, planning is forward-looking.

Perhaps the most conspicuous planning failure observed in recent weeks is the inadequacy of our nation's public health network. Of the nation's 3,000 public health agencies, only 20 percent have plans to cope with a biological attack, and the overwhelming majority are closed nights and weekends (Connolly 2001:11). Personnel and equipment problems also raise doubts about our nation's ability to respond to a bioterrorist attack (Stolberg 2001). Experts still disagree, sharply, on how to respond to anthrax exposure. Facing such uncertainty, the overwhelming majority of workers exposed to anthrax declined the federal government's offer to take an anthrax vaccine (Connolly 2002).

Another planning failure was the absence of a terrorism response or prevention plan in many of our nation's local communities. For example, the National League of Cities (2001) reported that 32 percent of all cities and 60 percent of small cities had no plan at all. Moreover, 52 percent of all cities and 68 percent of small cities reported no anti-terrorist training.

Chastened by concern over a possible outbreak of smallpox, the Centers for Disease Control and Prevention released a draft plan for that possibility late in November. The plan called for better awareness of smallpox by doctors, health officials, and the public so that any outbreak of the disease could be detected quickly (Gillis and Connolly 2001). Although the plan has its flaws and appears to be based on the assumption of an outbreak in a single city rather than multiple cities, it does represent an improvement over a previous plan promulgated in 1972.

In the aftermath of September 11, state and local governments have also devoted much more attention to planning, designing, or re-designing emergency response plans to cope with communications blackouts, public health epidemics, and other emergencies. Terrorism response or prevention plans are being drafted or reassessed, and specific measures are being taken to thwart a preventable attack. Governments and authorities in the New York City and Washington, D.C. areas have been particularly active. For example, the Washington area Metro authority removed all postal boxes and trash receptacles from Metro stops to make it easier to identify a suspicious package that might contain a chemical weapon or a bomb. In Salt Lake City, Utah, where the 2002 Winter Olympics were held, planning for security purposes has been extensive, thanks in part to additional assistance from the federal government (Shipley 2001).

The Indispensability of Coordination

The third element of the paradigm shift is growing recognition that coordination across government agencies is not a luxury but a necessity. Better coordination is needed both within policy domains (e.g., law enforcement) and across policy domains (law enforcement, public health, national security). Although few commentators or reformers would oppose coordination, it has not been high on our agenda in recent years.

When ambitious coordination efforts have been proposed, they have often floundered. Certainly, that has been true of proposed reorganizations that would have combined the FBI and the DEA into a single agency (Wilson 1989). More broadly, March and Olsen (1984) argue that administrative reorganization proposals have often been used as bargaining chips in debates that hinge more on substantive issues.

The creation of a new Office of Homeland Security, the decision to place that office in the White House, and the appointment of a prominent public official, Governor Tom Ridge of Pennsylvania, to head the office are all signs of the Bush administration's support for the principle of coordination. The decision to designate Ridge as the government's principal spokesperson on homeland security matters enhances the visibility of Ridge's office. It also helps to ensure that the executive branch speaks with some consistency on diverse threats to our security that fall within the jurisdiction of several cabinet departments.

A Well Informed and Informative Public

The mass media have made it possible for U.S. citizens (and others) to inform themselves more or less continuously of the latest developments in this horrible saga. CNN has so much news to offer that it supplements its news coverage with crisp bulletins that float steadily across the bottom of your television screen.

Public officials, for whatever combination of reasons, have often taken the position that the American people need to know in advance about threats that may or may not be credible. Thus Governor Gray Davis announced that Californians should be wary of bridge crossings. Attorney General John Ashcroft put the nation on general alert on October 29 without specifying the intended target or intended method (Eggen and Woodward; McGee 2001:15); Director of Homeland Security Tom Ridge issued a general alert on December 4, equally vague as to timing, method, and location (Dreazen and Fields 2001:20). Weaver would probably call these episodes classic examples of "blame avoidance" whereby politicians seek to escape electoral retribution if something goes badly wrong (Weaver 1986).

Although open government often facilitates greater accountability, this form of open government actually undermines it. By forecasting potential disaster whenever our intelligence gatherers discern disturbing portents, politicians help to extricate themselves from being held responsible for failure. However, like the boy who cried wolf, they may dull the public's sensitivity to a serious threat if one should actually materialize.

The government has attempted to enlist ordinary citizens as its eyes and ears. If you note any suspicious activities, we are told, you should inform your local law enforcement agency. And many Americans have responded. Within two months after September 11, the FBI's Internet Fraud Complaint Center, which invited browsers to report terrorist activity, received approximately 150,000 tips (Oldenburg 2001:C1). This is a new form of "fire-alarm" oversight (McCubbins and Schwartz 1984) more akin to communist systems, where citizens report on fellow citizens, than to a democracy where citizens are free to engage in odd behavior and to express unpopular sentiments.

Redundancy

Another key element of the new paradigm is the perception that for certain critical tasks we need to have parallel or redundant systems to ensure success. The most conspicuous example of this is an airport security system that involves intensive scrutiny of all passengers at the initial entry point, intensive scrutiny of a random sample of passengers at the gate, stricter rules concerning passenger conduct, and the presence of armed guards on many flights. The premise, as with other redundant systems, is that if one mechanism breaks down another will compensate for the failure (Landau 1969; Chisholm 1989).

The quest for redundant telecommunications systems is also well underway, though as a local government function it is proceeding more slowly. Dade County, Florida, for example, is hoping to obtain funds for a "hot" back-up site for its central computer system that would duplicate its mainframe facility and run parallel to it at another location; if the funds do not materialize, it will rely instead on a disaster-recovery site, where managers would work to restore data and get the system running again (Perlman 2001:40).

Redundancy, of course, adds to the overall cost of a system. Thus our new emphasis on redundancy, with upward pressure on the public treasury, clashes with a cost-cutting mentality that became embedded in 1981 and has guided most national politicians since that time.

ASSESSING THE NEW PARADIGM

What are we to make of the new paradigm that appears to be emerging in the wake of September 11? First, is it really new? Assuredly, some elements of it are quite familiar, evoking the New Deal, with its emphasis on planning and coordination conducted by a strong central government that enjoys the public's confidence and trust. In some respects, the new paradigm is one that Louis Brownlow might cheerfully have endorsed had he been asked to chair a presidential commission on terrorism in the 21st century. Yet, in other respects, the paradigm is new. The emphasis on public information and on public "snitching" is novel, as is the emphasis on redundancy to eliminate any possibility of error in critical sectors such as air transportation.

Second, is the new paradigm intellectually cohesive? In one sense, the answer is no. If, for example, one uses efficiency as one's criterion, it is possible to argue that redundancy undermines administrative efficiency and that a preference for government over the private sector threatens economic efficiency. On the other hand, efficiency is not the only litmus test for intellectual cohesiveness. In some respects, the elements of the new paradigm fit rather well together. For example, the steady flow of information between the government and the citizenry, with the mass media as intermediaries, provides a modicum of openness in a system that might otherwise seem oppressive.

Third, will the new paradigm last? As Kingdon (1995) has argued, opportunities for a policy innovation or a cluster of innovations arise when three "streams" converge: the problem stream, the policy stream, and the politics stream. The catastrophic destruction of the World Trade Centers and the partial destruction of the Pentagon dramatically altered perceptions of terrorism as a public problem. It was this change in the problem stream that triggered the new paradigm in the first place. Ironically, it might well be that another costly terrorist attack on U.S. soil is the surest way to guarantee that the new paradigm persists. If we invest heavily in preparations for additional terrorist attacks, and none materializes, policymakers and citizens may be tempted to conclude that the costs of planning and redundancy are not worth the effort.

THE NEW PARADIGM IN HISTORICAL PERSPECTIVE

How does the new paradigm compare to other ideas that have animated government reform efforts in recent years? Perhaps the most significant feature of the new paradigm is that it represents a significant departure from various forms of bureaucratic accountability that became institutionalized with the passage of legislation, the adoption of executive orders, and the acceptance of certain informal norms. Consider, for example, Light's (1997) account of the "tides of reform" that swept the United States during the 20th century. Three of these tides – the war on waste, the watchful eye, and liberation management – placed considerable emphasis on post hoc accountability, which the new paradigm would find unacceptable. Post hoc accountability implies that mistakes will be made but that they can be corrected. Planning and redundancy, in contrast, are rooted in the premise that errors need to be avoided in the first place.

Another way to think about the new paradigm is in terms of Kaufman's (1956) classic formulation of values in public administration. According to Kaufman, we began the 20th century enamored of representation, as exemplified by a strong Congress. The Progressive Era ushered in a period of admiration for "neutral competence" to be achieved through greater bureaucratic discretion (e.g., the independent regulatory commission). Subsequently, the New Deal inaugurated a period of support for strong leadership by the president. Although Kaufman did not directly comment on the late 20th century in his article, many scholars would agree that a quest for accountability and responsiveness marked the reform efforts of the late 20th century (Gormley 1989).

The new paradigm also differs from the latest series of reforms in public management, dubbed by Kettl (2000) the "global management revolution." According to Kettl, global management reform in several English-speaking countries has had six key characteristics: productivity, marketization, service orientation, decentralization, the ability to devise and track policy, and accountability for results. Clearly, some of these elements are incompatible with the central thrust of the new paradigm. Most conspicuously, marketization implies a lack of confidence in government, decentralization implies a lack of confidence in the federal government, and accountability for results implies a willingness to defer judgment until mistakes are made. The new paradigm, with its emphasis on trust in government, coordination by federal agencies, and planning, pushes public management in a very different direction.

Of course, it is important to stress that a new generation of government reforms seldom displaces the previous generation of reforms. Old reforms are not discarded but submerged. In this respect, governments resemble the nine layers of the city of Troy, with previous structures laying the foundation for new structures. Also, it is likely that some old-style reforms will continue to be adopted well into the new era that September 11 has inaugurated. For example, the education reform bill enacted into law in December 2001, with its emphasis on decentralization and accountability for results, has much more in common with Kettl's global management revolution than with the new paradigm I have outlined here.

IMPLICATIONS FOR PUBLIC MANAGEMENT RESEARCH

In my judgment, the changes in priorities wrought by the events of September 11 have three important implications for public management research over the next decade. First, we need to understand interorganizational coordination better. Second, we need to improve our capacity to create a "culture of trust" between agencies, between governments, and between the public and private sectors. Third, we need to develop a credible conception of what constitutes "acceptable risk" in a world that seems much riskier than the world we previously inhabited.

Networks and Partnerships

In recent years, students of public management and bureaucratic politics have devoted considerable attention to the relationship between political appointees and civil servants and to the relationship between politicians and bureaucracies. We have devoted more thought and empirical research to models of governance and to principal-agent theories. We have also studied the consequences of devolution to state and local governments and to privatization, especially contracts with for-profit firms and nonprofit organizations. And we have explored how to improve organizational results through performance measures, financial incentives, or both.

These research endeavors have been worthwhile. They have helped us to achieve accountability without sacrificing flexibility. They have helped us to identify opportunities to reconcile democratic values with Pareto optimality. They have helped us to move beyond the world of government agencies to appreciate the vital connections between agencies and politicians, agencies and judges, agencies and private contractors.

But we have paid a price for that progress, as we have largely ignored unresolved challenges of interorganizational coordination within government. How do we get federal agencies such as the FBI to share information with other federal agencies such as the Customs Service, the Coast Guard, and the Immigration and Naturalization Service? How do we get federal agencies such as the Department of Health and Human Services to integrate the disparate efforts of state and local public health agencies? How do we get agencies that toil in different sectors – national security agencies, law enforcement agencies, public health agencies, and emergency management agencies – to work together as if they were part of a seamless web?

The old answer to these questions – hierarchy – seems highly inappropriate in the wake of the global management revolution. To revert to a "command and control" approach would be to reverse a generation or two of reform efforts aimed at promoting teamwork through hortatory controls.

A better answer to these questions is networks. As understood by sociologists, networks are "unbounded or bounded clusters of organizations that ... are nonhierarchical collectives of legally separate units" (Alter and Hage 1993:46). Networks take many different forms and vary in their effectiveness (Provan and Milward 1995). They also differ in their formality, size, goals, and durability. Networks are more nimble and flexible than hierarchies; they are better able to adapt to changing circumstances.

The importance of networks to the challenges we face from world terrorists today is twofold: a network is the problem, and networks could be the solution. By all accounts, al Qaeda is a network or what Weick (1976) would call a "loosely coupled system." Highly decentralized, it relies on just-in-time information to avoid the danger of leaks. Individual cells within the network are highly autonomous (Zengerle 2001:20).

Whether we win the war against terrorism will depend on whether we manage to master the network as an institutional form. An effective law enforcement network is indispensable if we are to identify and apprehend terrorists. An effective public health network is essential if we are to cope with an outbreak of anthrax, smallpox, or some other life-threatening disease. An effective emergency response network is vital if we are to deal with explosives, chemical weapons, or other attacks that require a massive evacuation of personnel, the hospitalization of numerous victims, or some other crisis response.

Creating an effective network is not easy. Eugene Bardach (1998:263) puts it aptly when he quips that interagency collaboration is "an un-natural act committed by non-consenting adults." Because organization leaders and members are accustomed to pursuing their own organiza-tion's goals and standard operating procedures with little regard for the goals and practices of other organizations, we should not be surprised if interagency collaboration proves elusive. But it can and must be done if we are to anticipate and prevent most attacks and respond effectively to those attacks that nevertheless occur.

Culture of Trust

Organizational cooperation has many antecedents, but the key is to create a culture of trust. To prevent a disaster, how do we get law enforcement and public health and national security officials to share information and to seek a consensus on priorities, strategies, and tactics? If another disaster should occur, how do we get federal, state, and local agencies to coordinate without succumbing to territoriality and turf protection?

In *Taming the Bureaucracy* (Gormley 1989), I argued that "hortatory" and "catalytic" controls usually prove more effective than "coercive" controls when trying to influence a bureaucracy. If this is true for politi-cians and judges, it is also true for other bureaucracies, whether perched in the same level of government or a different one.

Alter and Hage (1993:141-143) believe that two counties in New York state were successful in creating a culture of trust for hospice care. They attribute this success to a diversified resource base, a combination of local autonomy and commitment, and a highly professional core coordinating agency.

Bardach (1998:134) believes that technical clarity helps to foster collaboration. He adds that interagency task force managers should engage in gestures that remind participants of what binds them together. For example, a San Mateo County task force on children began a meeting with members passing around photos from their respective childhoods; the same group was served peanut butter and jelly sandwiches for lunch to strengthen their resolve to act on behalf of young children (Bardach 1998:266).

Acceptable Risk

We live in a world that seems much riskier than the world we knew before September 11. In its response to the terrorist attacks, the U.S. government has sought to extinguish some risks altogether while reducing other risks and downplaying still other risks. It is not clear that we have struck the right balance.

For example, we have invested heavily in airport security. Fortified cockpits, federal marshalls accompanying flights, random searches of passengers at the gate, and electronic or personal searches of all luggage are costly improvements. The purchase of 2,000 explosive detection machines alone has an estimated price tag of $2 billion (Nakashima and Schneider 2001).

At the same time, we have done far less to cope with threats to our nation's seaports, which are arguably even more vulnerable at the present time. For example, the U.S. Customs Service inspects only about 2 percent of the 14 million containers arriving in the United States every year (Booth 2002). Chemical plants with large amounts of ammonia, chlorine, ethylene oxide, and other hazardous chemicals have also received limited attention, despite the fact that at least 123 plants keep amounts of toxic chemicals that, if released, could endanger more than 1 million people (Grimaldi and Gugliotta 2001).

It is easy to understand why we have invested so much in air transportation security and so little in other threats to public safety. The terrorist hijackings of September 11 claimed the lives of over 3,000 people. Air travel is vital to both national and international commerce, and air transportation is the preferred means of travel for citizens traveling long distances for pleasure. These factors help to explain Secretary of Transportation Norman Mineta's (2001) pledge "to ensure American passengers are provided with the highest possible levels of safety."

In fact, if the highest possible level of safety means zero risk, that is not a realistic alternative. To eliminate risk altogether would mean to eliminate flying altogether, which no one is prepared to do. A more reasonable standard would be to pursue a high level of safety, with minimal risk (e.g., perhaps one death for every 1 million flights). Even here though, we need to keep the costs of safe air travel in mind. The virtual elimination of one risk, such as the risk of another hijacked airplane's being used as a lethal weapon, may make it more difficult for us to avoid some other major risk, such as arson at a chemical plant, with many thousands of casualties. Indeed, many experts believe that the next major terrorist attack on U.S. soil will not try to replicate the September 11 assault but rather will utilize a different strategy altogether.

Some government agencies are already accustomed to dealing with risk. The U.S. EPA, for example, has conducted systematic risk assessments for hazardous waste and drinking water contaminants since the 1970s (Andrews 1999:266). But it is not clear that the EPA has gotten this right. For example, the EPA does a much better job of assessing cancer risks than non-cancer risks; more broadly, it does a much better job of assessing human health risks than ecological risks. Another problem is that the EPA sometimes exaggerates the precision of its knowledge – e.g., by releasing a point estimate for risk when a range of estimates would be more accurate (National Academy of Public Administration 1995:41-42).

For public managers at other agencies, as at the EPA, a key challenge is to develop risk assessments that are precise enough to be helpful but imprecise enough to be credible. Another key challenge is to integrate risk assessments with statutory requirements, political pressures, and public expectations. Lay persons and experts often rate risks quite differently, with lay judgments being shaped by the ease with which they can call a particular risk to mind (Slovic et al. 1990). This phenomenon, known as the "availability heuristic," means that the perceived risk of a flood (or a terrorist hijacking) increases sharply after the incidence of a flood (or a terrorist hijacking). If given significant weight, the availability heuristic results in a poor allocation of resources.

One useful framework for thinking systematically about risk comes from Morone and Woodward (1986), who outline several strategies for regulating risky technologies. Their strategies include: prohibition, limits on use, prevention, containment, and mitigation. As they note (Morone and Woodward 1986:127), prohibition is seldom an option and mitigation is seldom effective enough, leaving the intermediate strategies as the more appealing ones. At least two of these strategies have been employed in addressing air safety threats since September 11. Prevention, through intensive security clearance processes, is the primary strategy; limits on use, such as severe restrictions on general aviation, is a secondary strategy.

CONCLUSION

The terrorist threat to our nation's security is both insidious and diffuse. Unlike more conventional threats from nation states, it is difficult to pinpoint and difficult to control. Like the shift in pollution threats from point sources, such as power plants, to non-point sources, such as farm runoff, it requires radical adjustments in our thinking, new management practices, and additional resources.

In this paper, I have sketched the rough outlines of a new paradigm that seems to be emerging in response to the events of September 11. Its key elements are trust in government, the revival of planning, the indispensability of coordination, a well-informed and informing public, and redundancy. If this new paradigm takes root, we can expect some important consequences to flow from it, including a larger public sector, a greater emphasis on anticipation and prevention, and keener interest in the development of effective networks and partnerships between governments, between agencies, and between the public and private sectors. The quest for post hoc accountability, which animated so many government reform initiatives in the late 20th century, will undoubtedly persist but will no longer suffice. One thing is certain: as the stakes get higher and the risks of a catastrophe escalate, we will need to develop a better system of governance than the one we possess today.

ACKNOWLEDGEMENTS

The author would like to thank Ted Gayer and Patrick Wolf for helpful comments on an early draft of this paper.

REFERENCES

Adams, Richard. 1972. *Watership Down*. New York: MacMillan & Co.

Alter, Catherine and Jerald Hage. 1993. *Organizations Working Together*. Beverly Hills: Sage Publications.

Andrews, Richard. 1999. *Managing the Environment, Managing Ourselves*. New Haven: Yale University Press.

Bardach, Eugene. 1998. *Getting Agencies to Work Together: The Practice and Theory of Managerial Craftsmanship*. Washington, D.C.: Brookings.

Booth, William. 2002. "Where Sea Meets Shore, Scenarios for Terrorists," *Washington Post*, January 2.

Chisholm, Donald. 1989. *Coordination Without Hierarchy: Informal Structures in Multiorganizational Systems*. Berkeley: University of California Press.

Connolly, Ceci. 2001. "Bioterrorism Defense Plan Called Inadequate," *Washington Post*, October 22, p. 11.

Connolly, Ceci. 2002. "Workers Exposed to Anthrax Shun Vaccine," *Washington Post*, January 8, p. 6.

Dreazen, Yochi and Gary Fields. 2001. "Ridge Issues New Terrorist-Attack Alert, Warning of a Possible Strike This Month," *Wall Street Journal*, December 4, p. 20.

Eggen, Dan and Bob Woodward. 2001. "FBI Issues 2nd Global Attack Alert," *Washington Post*, October 30, p. 1.

Gallup Research Center of the University of Nebraska-Lincoln. 2001. Presentation on "Public Opinion in the Aftermath of September 11," Washington, D.C., The Gallup Building, November 27.

Gillis, Justin and Ceci Connolly. 2001. "U.S. Details Response to Smallpox," *Washington Post*, November 27, 2001, p. 1.

Gormley, William, Jr. 1989. *Taming the Bureaucracy: Muscles, Prayers, and Other Strategies*. Princeton: Princeton University Press.

Grimaldi, James and Guy Gugliotta. 2001. "Chemical Plants Are Feared as Targets," *Washington Post*, December 16, p. 1.

Kaufman, Herbert. 1956. "Emerging Conflicts in the Doctrine of Public Administration," *American Political Science Review* 50 (December), pp. 1,057-1,073.

Kettl, Donald. 2000. *The Global Management Revolution: A Report on the Transformation of Governance.* Washington, D.C.: Brookings.

Kingdon, John. 1995. *Agendas, Alternatives, and Public Policies,* 2nd ed. New York: Harper Collins.

Landau, Martin. 1969. "Redundancy, Rationality, and the Problem of Duplication and Overlap," *Public Administration Review* 29, pp. 346-358.

Light, Paul. 1997. *The Tides of Reform: Making Government Work, 1945-1995.* New Haven: Yale University Press.

March, James and Johan Olsen. 1984. "The New Institutionalism: Organizational Factors in Political Life," *American Political Science Review* 78, pp. 734-749.

McCubbins, Mathew and Thomas Schwartz. 1984. "Congressional Oversight Overlooked: Police Patrols versus Fire Alarms," *American Journal of Political Science* 28 (February), pp. 165-179.

McGee, Jim. 2001. "Some Senior FBI Officials Opposed Issuing Oct. 29 Alert," *Washington Post,* November 10, p. 15.

Mineta, Norman. 2001. Statement before the Committee on Appropriations, Subcommittee on Transportation, U.S. Senate, September 20.

Morone, Joseph and Edward Woodhouse. 1986. *Averting Catastrophe: Strategies for Regulating Risky Technologies.* Berkeley: University of California Press.

Nakashima, Ellen and Greg Schneider. 2001. "U.S. Likely to Miss Goal on Screening," *Washington Post,* November 28, p. 1.

National Academy of Public Administration. 1995. *Setting Priorities, Getting Results: A New Direction for EPA.* Washington, D.C.: author.

National League of Cities. 2001. "Most Cities Have Terrorism Readiness Plans, But Many Will Reassess and Tighten Security." Washington, D.C.: NLC Press Release, September 25. Source: http://www.nlc.org.

Oldenburg, Dan. 2001. "The FBI Spins Its Terrorism Web," *Washington Post*, November 15, p. C1.

Perlman, Ellen. 2001. "IT in the Ruins," *Governing*, November, pp. 38-41.

Provan, Keith and H. Brinton Milward. 1995. "A Preliminary Theory of Interorganizational Network Effectiveness: A Comparative Study of Four Community Mental Health Systems," *Administrative Science Quarterly* 40 (March), pp. 1-33.

Shipley, Amy. 2001. "In Salt Lake, Security Is an Olympic Task," *Washington Post*, December 23, p. 1.

Slovic, Paul, Baruch Fischhoff, and Sarah Lichtenstein. 1990. "Rating the Risks." In Theodore Glickman and Michael Gough, eds., *Readings in Risk*. Washington, D.C.: Resources for the Future, pp. 61-74.

Stolberg, Sheryl Gay. 2001. "Some Experts Say U.S. is Vulnerable to a Germ Attack," *New York Times* September 30, p. 1.

Weaver, R. Kent. 1986. "The Politics of Blame Avoidance," *Journal of Public Policy* 6, pp. 371-398.

Weick, Karl. 1976. "Educational Organizations as Loosely Coupled Systems," *Administrative Science Quarterly* 21 (March), pp. 1-19.

Wilson, James Q. 1989. *Bureaucracy: What Government Agencies Do and Why They Do It*. New York: Basic Books.

Zengerle, Jason. 2001. "Police Blotter: What the FBI Is Doing Wrong," *The New Republic*, December 31, pp. 20-23.

DEFENDING AGAINST THE APOCALYPSE: THE LIMITS OF HOMELAND SECURITY

Michael Barkun

The September 11 attacks were not simply destructive of lives and buildings. They inflicted profound psychic damage – damage that must be understood if we are to grasp the connections between terrorism and governmental responses. The inner psychological trauma of September 11 was initially linked to shocking images, planes crashing into buildings, occupants jumping to their deaths, and landmark structures collapsing as panicked crowds sought to outrun clouds of debris.

Much of this was seen in real time by immense television audiences. The consequence was to redefine the scope of the events. They instantly became national, indeed international, with vast numbers of vicarious victims. The effect of mass communications in this case, as in the assassination of John Kennedy nearly four decades earlier, was to transform spectators into survivors.

The imagery of September 11 was not simply shocking or frightening. It was apocalyptic, for it seemed to manifest world-destroying power. The very name given to the World Trade Center site – "ground zero" – came from the lexicon of nuclear weapons, themselves associated with the capacity to destroy civilization. Such connections were quickly grasped by religious millennialists. John Hagee, a San Antonio evangelist, watched the television coverage and, as he put it, "recognized that the Third World War had begun and that it would escalate from this day until the Battle of Armageddon." An Internet book service patronized by Protestant fundamentalists polled its customers and found that 65 percent thought the "war on terrorism" was preparing the way for the end-times.

These millenarian associations were reinforced by the attackers themselves, acting from religious motivations, and by their presumed mentor, Osama bin Laden, who combined messianic pretensions with a claim that terrorism is part of an ongoing war between believers and infidels.

But these apocalyptic associations were not limited to religionists. The television images triggered instant references to secular popular culture. In a widely reported interview, the film director Robert Altman observed: "Nobody would have thought to commit an atrocity like that unless they'd seen it in a movie." In fact, urban cataclysms had long been staples of both popular fiction and motion pictures, expressions of what Susan Sontag has called "the imagination of disaster." Thus Stephen Vincent Benet's 1937 short story, "By the Waters of Babylon," described a desolated future Manhattan of empty ruins.

Such ideas transferred readily to film, especially after World War II demonstrated that cities could in fact be obliterated. By the 1950s, disaster films had become a virtual genre, but as each new calamity numbed the viewer, it became necessary to depict ever more lurid future catastrophes. Thus, for witnesses to September 11, the TV images fused with internalized images from fiction and film.

If the 9-11 attacks were characterized by the vividness of the imagery, the anthrax outbreak was precisely opposite. While some envelopes clearly contained powdered anthrax spores, a number of cases occurred without any visually identifiable disease agent. It scarcely mattered that there were only 23 cases, resulting in five deaths, or that no evidence existed linking the anthrax perpetrators with al Qaeda. In the popular mind, the anthrax outbreak became an extension of the September 11 "story." Now evil too painful to watch was followed by evil that could not be seen. The dramatically visible was followed by the dramatically invisible, the more unnerving for its very invisibility.

What, then, are the implications for what we now term "homeland security?" In the first place, the events have, as I have suggested, played themselves out on two levels: one has been the level of physical destruction that might be quantified in terms of deaths and injuries, persons infected, jobs lost, buildings destroyed. The other has been the level of perception, played out in the minds of millions of Americans. And, as Jessica Stern noted well before these events, one of the dilemmas of government is whether policy decisions should be based on the one or the other: "In other words," she asks, "should dangers that evoke disproportionate fears receive disproportionate resources?" And what, indeed, does "disproportionate" itself mean in a political system that is supposed to be responsive to the expressed desires of the electorate and where few standards exist for establishing proportionality?

There are also problems of feasibility. Thirty years ago, Hannah Arendt suggested that civilian populations could no longer be defended, a change that compromises the very purpose of military organizations. Defense might still be possible through such indirect mechanisms as deterrence, proxy wars, or pre-emptive attacks, but large armed forces themselves do not necessarily confer security on a state's citizens. Arendt attributed these changes to the invention of weapons of mass destruction that could be used with little or no warning time.

However, the World Trade Center attack was a mass casualty event not produced by weapons of mass destruction, as these have traditionally been understood. Rather, immense destruction was achieved with weapons no more exotic than the box cutters required to commandeer the aircraft. If one excludes the emergency workers drawn by the attack, the dead were fortuitous victims – present by virtue of an airplane ticket or a job. Their – and our – vulnerability reflects what Harold Lasswell called the "socialization of danger," in which the risk of attack is no longer primarily borne by military personnel. Weapons may be indiscriminate, adversaries may deliberately target civilians, and, as has already been noted, the ability of the military to defend civilians has become problematic.

It is not even clear where the dangers lie. Thomas Friedman said the 9-11 attacks were not so much failures of intelligence as they were failures of imagination. Few had previously considered the use of fully fueled civilian airliners as missiles. Where warfare could once be analyzed in terms of relatively fixed categories of weapons and tactics, we now face a world filled with dangers that we may not be able to conceive. In such a world where "all things are possible," the capacity to adjust to new possibilities necessarily falls behind. It is difficult to create contingency plans for inconceivable contingencies.

At the same time, the pressure on authorities to "do something" cannot be resisted. Thus there has been anti-terrorism legislation on an almost yearly basis. There is little evidence that these measures significantly reduced the danger, but they did serve as exercises in symbolic politics to soothe an anxious public.

Such efforts began again shortly after September 11 with the creation of an Office of Homeland Security. These efforts are ongoing, and while their full development has not yet taken place, the possibilities are already evident.

From the president's initial comments, it became commonplace to refer to the attacks as "acts of war." The conflict in Afghanistan reinforced this tendency. However, classifying the attacks and the response in terms of armed conflict significantly oversimplifies both public and official reactions. While the analogy to war surely captures much of contemporary perceptions, it also misses a significant element – namely, the extent to which these events have also simultaneously taken on the attributes of "disasters," with consequences similar to those of more conventional fires, plane crashes, and natural calamities. These attributes have colored our perceptions of terrorism as well as actual and proposed governmental responses to it. We have come to view the events of September 11 and the ensuing anthrax outbreak as both "acts of war" *and* "disasters." Indeed, as we shall see, it is precisely the mingling of the two categories that makes "homeland security" so problematic.

Some researchers have tried to define "disaster" in terms of some threshold level of destruction. However, these efforts have been unsatisfactory, because limited physical destruction sometimes produces the same responses as much broader devastation (as, for example, after the assassination of President Kennedy); and because large-scale destruction does not always evoke reactions proportionate to the damage (as, for example, in the case of the influenza epidemic of 1918).

In the end, "disaster" is better understood as a mental construct that people place on experience. What matter most may be the prevailing sense of vulnerability, the adequacy of available explanations of misfortune, and a society's representations of death and destruction. Depending upon these factors, some collective-stress events are perceived as "disasters," while others may be borne with a stoic sense of the vicissitudes of life. Events as dissimilar as the World Trade Center attack and the anthrax outbreak may be similarly categorized despite enormous differences in the scope of damage.

Over the last hundred years, an important shift has occurred in the popular conceptualization of disaster. Natural disasters – earthquakes, hurricanes, and the like – have shrunk in significance. This is a consequence of improvements in prediction, explanation, protection, and emergency response. While they still present dangers, they do not call forth the same fears that they once did. Their place has been taken by manmade disasters, a litany of which can be readily constructed: from Bhopal, to Chernobyl, to September 11.

An important characteristic of manmade disasters is their potential unboundedness. Unlike natural disasters, which tend to recur in much the same ways, manmade disasters can be distinctively different from one another, because of alterations in technology and in the motives of perpetrators. It is difficult to predict either their spatial or temporal limits. The connecting links among individuals and nations – highways, power grids, information networks, and so on – make possible not only the sharing of benefits but the expansion of risks. Dangers pass from the impact area along spreading lines of contact. It is difficult to isolate a manmade disaster in such a world of interdependencies.

Insofar as recent terrorism is concerned, we are therefore in the process of blurring the line between "attack" and "disaster," with profound policy implications. To the extent that we understood September 11 as an "attack," it was an "act of war" that implied a military response. That response began in Afghanistan on October 7th, and at this writing, is now moving toward a conclusion. To the extent that we understood September 11 as a "disaster," that implied a civilian emergency response. As in disasters generally, the "first responders" to the World Trade Center were civilian police, firemen, and rescue workers. They took casualties far heavier than those so far borne by U.S. military personnel in Afghanistan.

One can, of course, argue that the dual military and civilian responses were dictated by characteristics of the situation. The political agenda of the hijackers, and al Qaeda's presence in Afghanistan, mandated a projection of American military power, while the immediate needs at the World Trade Center and the Pentagon automatically activated the appropriate civilian agencies.

However, the combination of attack/response and disaster/response had begun to appear in counter-terrorism policy proposals before September 11, so that 9-11 merely reinforced existing predispositions.

A proposal to combine the two was offered almost exactly a year ago in the final report of the United States Commission on National Security in the 21st Century, better known by the names of its co-chairs, Gary Hart and Warren Rudman. The Hart-Rudman Commission can hardly be faulted for lack of foresight, for it predicted, "A direct attack against American citizens *on American soil* is likely over the next quarter century." Their central proposal was for the creation of a cabinet-level National Homeland Security Agency (NHSA). The core of the new agency would be the existing Federal Emergency Management Agency (FEMA), augmented by the Customs Service, Border Patrol, Coast Guard, National Infrastructure Protection Center, and a number of other units presently housed elsewhere. In addition, the new NHSA would have close links with the Department of Defense through a new Assistant Secretary of Defense for Homeland Security and a reconfigured National Guard. The latter would take on "homeland security" as its primary mission. Department of Defense involvement would also take the form of a Joint Task Force with responsibilities for the integration of homeland security concerns into training, doctrine, and command and control. Much of this proposed reorganization had already been embodied in pending legislation when the September 11 attacks occurred.

The proposals promised an end to the redundancies and turf wars of the present jurisdictional patchwork. The proposals' attractiveness, originally based on their organizational rationality, has now been reinforced by the fears of an anxious and vulnerable public.

Such a fusion of national defense with disaster preparedness has already been implemented in some European countries, notably in Sweden. Under the Swedish model, "national security" has been reconceptualized to cover emergencies that range from natural disasters and industrial accidents to military attacks. This conscious blurring of the line between military and civilian emergency response appears to reflect the circumstances of a small, unitary state whose population is highly concentrated in a few urban areas, and whose military establishment is in search of a post-Cold War mission.

The implications of such a model for the United States are quite different, given the differences in scale, political structure, and international role. In addition, events like those of September 11 present special challenges in terms of policy implications.

As I hope my earlier remarks made clear, the perception of recent events is more powerful than any objective damage assessment. Indeed, as a practical matter, in this case as in other crisis situations, perception *is* reality. That being so, the result is a disturbing paradox: the overwhelming magnitude of the perceived danger – what I earlier referred to as its apocalyptic quality – appears to mandate an immediate and radical response. Yet even the most dramatic mobilization of capacities cannot produce the total security most people desire. If the goal is the complete elimination of a terrorist threat on American soil, even the most draconian measures will fail. We have yet, as a society, to face the question of what level of risk is acceptable. Just as we recoil from the need to allocate scarce medical resources, so we avoid the question of the level of safety that is practical and acceptable. Further, there is good reason to believe that whatever added security is purchased will be paid for in disturbing unintended consequences.

Ironically, counter-terrorism proposals based on the fusion of war and disaster may well stimulate the very violence they seek to avoid. The American radical right has long feared a tyrannical regime built around the Federal Emergency Management Agency. The FEMA rumors are a staple of militias' subculture, whose members believe the federal government will concoct a crisis to provide the pretext. Indeed, some right-wing Web sites have already speculated that the September 11 attacks were staged for just this reason. To the extent that homeland security proposals link disaster response with national security, they unknowingly play to precisely these paranoid fantasies. The unfortunate result is likely to be an upsurge in domestic terrorism as a byproduct of defense against transnational terrorism.

Intrinsic to many homeland security proposals is a revision of existing civil-military relationships. Whether the issue is drug trafficking or civil disorder, the armed forces have been viewed as the resource of last resort. The current presence of armed and uniformed National Guard personnel at airport security checkpoints is merely the most recent manifestation of this tendency. The traditional barrier to military involvement in domestic law enforcement, the post-Civil War Posse Comitatus Act, has been significantly loosened by recent amendments, and may well be altered further.

At the end of the Second World War, the constitutional scholar Edward S. Corwin voiced similar misgivings when he noted that "the restrictive clauses of the Constitution are not, *as to the citizen at least*, automatically suspended, but the scope of the rights to which they extend is capable of being reduced in face of the urgencies of war, sometimes even to the vanishing point, depending on the demands of the war."

Such fears might appear overblown if the crisis were seen to have clear boundaries. In Britain during World War I, the expression "for the duration" gained currency as shorthand for the period until the war ended. The same idiom returned in both Britain and the United States during World War II, with the same meaning. It made intuitive sense precisely because, as conventional wars, the two world wars were expected to, and did in fact have, clear beginnings and conclusions, ending when one set of belligerents sued for peace.

The present situation, however, is not of that kind. Indeed, from the president on down, high officials have been at pains to warn that the war against terrorism will be a struggle of uncertain length. Hence measures of an emergency character imply a more open-ended commitment than those in previous conflicts. To the extent that war and disaster have been conflated, the war against terrorism partakes of the unboundedness of manmade disaster, the inability to predict targets, weapons, or consequences; hence the inability to place clear limits on the defensive means that might be employed.

The idea of an open-ended "war on terrorism" links the old conception of war-as-armed-conflict with more recent metaphorical usages, such as the "war on poverty" and the "war on drugs." Unlike the latter, however, the present struggle can potentially result in a permanent condition of domestic vigilance institutionalized in law and practice.

Such an outcome is made more likely by the contemporary overlapping of "war" and "disaster." It implies that all forms of emergency response must be linked, whether civilian or military, national or local. This potential breaching of boundaries between types of response mirrors the breaching of conventional boundaries among types of threats. Thus, there are no longer clear distinctions between war and peace, war and crime, and war and disaster. Rather, myriad forms of "low-intensity" conflict inhabit a transitional zone of ambiguous events.

The temptation to follow these changes with parallel alterations in governance is considerable, yet in my view need to be resisted. In the first place, they threaten to radically destabilize the federal system by shifting law enforcement responsibilities, traditionally state functions, toward the national government. As some conservative lawyers have already pointed out, this may not only jeopardize constitutional arrangements but may also be bad counter-terrorism policy, inasmuch as complex systems are better protected by redundancy than by centralization.

Second, by combining disaster-response with an open-ended war on terrorism, advocates of proposals such as those of Hart-Rudman in effect routinize emergency. The notion of routinized emergency may seem oxymoronic until we remember that, like "disaster," "emergency" is a construction placed on the world rather than an objective condition. Homeland security arrangements that make emergency a chronic condition, whether by invoking war, disaster, or both, bring to mind Alexander Hamilton's warning in Federalist #8:

> The violent destruction of life and property incident to war, the continual effort and alarm attendant on a state of continual danger, will compel nations the most attached to liberty to resort for repose and security to institutions which have a tendency to destroy their civil and political rights. To be more safe, they at length become willing to run the risk of being less free.

Dangers of this type flow from the inability to discriminate between law enforcement problems and national security problems. A small foretaste of the difficulties has been presented in the debate about the appropriate forum for trying those suspected of involvement with al Qaeda. However, issues of classification spill over into problems of governance, for if a problem is understood to be one of national security, government will be given far more latitude than if the problem is regarded as one of law enforcement. The tendency has been to discuss the issue as if it were primarily one of moral judgment: in this view, the "law enforcement" label is seen as misplaced because it allegedly reduces the seriousness of the offense or gives to the offender rights that he does not deserve. In contrast, "national security" signals the total mobilization of available resources against enemies to whom one owes relatively little. However, the issue is less one of providing just desserts to malefactors than it is of preserving necessary restraints on the exercise of power.

As Hamilton recognized, national security imperatives, which imply that the survival of the society may be at stake, can legitimize a wide range of exceptions from normal political and legal practice. It was those exceptions that Harold Lasswell had in mind when he wrote his influential and prescient 1941 essay, "The Garrison State." That is a state, Lasswell said, dominated by those he called "the specialists on violence." While he had military personnel primarily in mind, he noted that in technologically and organizationally complex societies, specialists on violence would also have to possess a significant array of civilian managerial skills. Homeland security measures predicated on a fusion of disaster preparedness and military defense require precisely that sense of routinized, chronic emergencies that form the basis for the garrison state.

The danger posed by such a governmental reorientation is greatly lessened when the emergency is brief, and where an idiom like "the duration" remains meaningful. However, clear boundaries are precisely what modern terrorism lacks. It cannot be definitively tied to a territorial base. Rooting al Qaeda out of Afghanistan does not prevent its re-emergence elsewhere. These are, to some extent, "acephalous" organizations, unlikely to have a single "head" whose removal will immobilize the constituent cells. Because such organizations operate in secrecy, it is difficult to be sure of their size, resources, or intentions. As a result, the capabilities of terrorist groups are far more likely to be over-estimated than under-estimated.

Despite the wish to take account of worst-case scenarios, there are substantial reasons to avoid responding by institutionalizing major changes in governance.

First, we have been without a clear enemy for 10 years, ever since the Soviet Union collapsed. While that was the cause for rejoicing, it also deprived the West of a moral vision of a struggle between good and evil that had persisted since the late 1940s. For more than 40 years, our sense of national identity was closely linked to the presence and hostility of the Soviet Union. Once the threat was removed, the world and our place in it became at once confusing and blurred. Osama bin Laden has restored the sense of foreign policy as a struggle between the forces of light and the forces of darkness, but the fact that such simplicity is psychologically comforting does not mean that it should be the basis for far-reaching structural changes.

Second, there is as yet no evidence that any proposed homeland security measures will in fact produce greater security, although they may well create the perception of greater security in the same manner as the troops at airport security checkpoints. The fact that we may feel more secure must be distinguished from any actual reduction in terrorist incidents.

Third, many of the recent and proposed changes have been most strongly driven by fear of weapons of mass destruction. Bin Laden and his circle have clearly been interested in such weapons (as, by the way, have some domestic extremists). It hardly needs emphasizing that we must prevent if at all possible their acquisition of nuclear, radiological, biological, or chemical weapons. Fortunately, however, these weapons tend to be extremely difficult to obtain, maintain, and utilize. Against this one must weigh the fact that even very modest casualties, such as those produced by the anthrax mailings, can provoke high levels of fear.

If I end on a note of uncertainty, it is because so much remains uncertain. Since that is the case, the one conclusion that seems inescapable is this: the temptation to launch broad, systemic changes should be resisted, both because they may not do good and because they may do harm. Instead, a more prudent path is that of incremental experimentation, where outcomes can be monitored, approaches modified, and initiatives developed. While this may lack the immediate political appeal of the "grand gesture," it suggests a strategy more conducive to long-term safety.

MISSION IMPOSSIBLE? THE WHITE HOUSE OFFICE OF HOMELAND SECURITY

Michael A. Wermuth

PREFACE

This paper explores the history, authorities, structure, and potential limitations of the Office of Homeland Security, established by the president following the attacks of September 11, 2002. It questions whether the authority of that office is sufficient to effect the necessary discipline into the federal bureaucracy and provide the mechanism for close working relationships with states and localities for a national approach to combating terrorism.

The views expressed in this paper are those of the author and do not necessarily reflect the views or policies of RAND or its clients or sponsors.

HISTORICAL CONTEXT

The prior administration had attempted, through executive action,[1] to establish a process for implementing executive branch programs for combating terrorism. The executive orders vested in the attorney general the responsibility for "crisis management" and for "consequence management" in the director of the Federal Emergency Management Agency (FEMA), and created an interagency coordinating mechanism led by designated individuals on the National Security Council staff. The results were the establishment of numerous coordinating committees and subcommittees and a series of seemingly endless meetings – all of which did little more than try to execute existing programs and practically nothing to formulate strategy, policy, or budget priorities for developing and executing a national approach for combating terrorism more effectively.

The Bush Administration was quick to recognize that the existing structure and mechanisms were not fully effective, but did not move as rapidly as some had hoped to implement better ones. The administration resisted various congressional attempts in the early spring of last year to send key officials to appear before committees of jurisdiction to articulate its new program for combating terrorism. In exchange, the White House agreed to a set of Senate hearings in early May, highlighting the top officials of the responsible Cabinet agencies,[2] to provide collectively the administration position on the issue. Attempts to create a new structure and process by executive order had proven to be unsuccessful in the weeks leading up to those hearings. In a May 8 statement – right in the middle of the hearings – the president directed the vice president "to oversee the development of a coordinated national effort" to review the entire issue and to recommend changes in administration policy and structure. In that same statement, the president authorized the director of FEMA to establish an "Office on National Preparedness," to "coordinate all federal programs dealing with weapons of mass destruction, consequence management within the departments of defense, health and human services, justice, and energy, the Environmental Protection Agency, and other federal agencies."[3] Over the course of last summer, the vice president and his staff undertook a review of the reports of various commissions and other entities that had specifically addressed the related policy and structure issues,[4] as well as pending legislation in the Congress, with a view toward making recommendations for improvements to the president in the fall.

September 11 upset the timetable of the vice president's deliberative process and the plans for FEMA to have a larger role. In his address to the Congress and the nation on September 20, the president announced his selection of then-governor of Pennsylvania Tom Ridge – a close political confidant and supporter – to head the administration's "homeland security" efforts. By executive order of October 8, the president established, within the Executive Office of the President, the Office of Homeland Security,[5] with Ridge at its helm.

THE DEFINITIONAL ISSUE

The phrase "homeland security" suffers from the same defect as many other terms in the field of terrorism – "crisis management," "consequence management," and "weapons of mass destruction," to mention a few. None is clearly defined, and there are conflicting definitions of such terms. (There is, in fact, no universally accepted definition of *terrorism* itself, not even a standard one for the federal government.) Is defense of the United States from ballistic missile attack part of "homeland security?" Is stopping illegal drugs from entering our country an element of "homeland security?"[6] In each case, it could logically be so argued.

It is unfortunate that the executive order establishing the Office of Homeland Security does not explicitly define the term. The places where it may come close are in the "mission" and "functions" sections,[7] and in the section amending an earlier executive order dealing with the execution of national security responsibilities in the executive branch, stating there that the office and its related Homeland Security Council – to distinguish the responsibilities from those of the National Security Council – are responsible for policy for "terrorist threats and attacks inside the United States."[8]

THE AUTHORITY ISSUES

The mission of the Office of Homeland Security is relatively straightforward. It is:

[T]o develop and coordinate the implementation of a comprehensive national strategy to secure the United States from terrorist threats or attacks. . . [and to] perform the functions necessary to carry out this mission.[9]

The executive order generally describes the functions of the office to be "to coordinate the executive branch's efforts to detect, prepare for, prevent, protect against, respond to, and recover from terrorist attacks within the United States."[10] In successive subsections, the order then describes in some detail the responsibilities of the office in each of those categories. In doing so, it uses the word "coordinate" or "coordinating" a total of 37 times,[11] but the word *direct* appears nowhere within the authorities or responsibilities of the office. It is generally accepted that Tom Ridge has a close professional relationship with the president. From that standpoint, Director Ridge may well be able to persuade the president to direct other officials to do or refrain from doing certain things. It is also likely that no department or agency head will want to be seen – at least in the near term –as not cooperating with his office in developing or implementing administration policy or programs for combating terrorism. Nevertheless, the question arises whether it would be better if that office were given some explicit authority to direct certain activities within and among various federal agencies.

One specific area where the office may lack the necessary "teeth" is in the budget arena. The executive order does not give the director any budget control mechanisms. It only provides a process for the office to "review and provide advice to the heads of departments and agencies" on their respective programs and to "provide advice to the director [of the Office of Management and Budget] on the level and use of funding in departments and agencies" and whether funding levels are "necessary and appropriate" for homeland security-related activities. Absent the specific authority to implement some specific budget controls – direct budget decertification, funds sequester, directed reprogramming – it is doubtful that the office can have any significant long-term influence on federal program priorities.

Compare the budget authority of this office to the Office of National Drug Control Policy (ONDCP). Scholars, policymakers, the media, and rank-and-file citizens can disagree about the effectiveness of ONDCP in reducing the trafficking and use of illegal drugs. What cannot be fairly argued is whether ONDCP has strong budget authority to help further its mandate. That authority is statutory[12] and provides for the decertification of budgets of non-complying departments and agencies. The existence of that authority and the prospect of its use have essentially been sufficient to create the necessary atmosphere for compromise between the various agencies and ONDCP. The "proof" for that proposition: the decertification authority has only been used fully one time, and while ONDCP did not get everything it was seeking, it got most of it.

Members of Congress and others have suggested that the Office of Homeland Security should have a statutory basis for its authorities, including certain budget controls, in the same way, perhaps in different detail, that exists for ONDCP, and that its head should be subject to Senate confirmation.[13] So far, there appears to be a willingness among members not to push the issue until they see how the office will work under the authority of the executive order.

AN EXAMPLE: THE BORDER CONTROL ISSUE

What does the lack of directory and budgetary authority mean in practical terms? Consider the issue of improving enforcement of the various laws and regulations at our borders.

The Hart-Rudman Commission was on the right track when it recommended in its phase three report[14] the formation of a new entity, a significant responsibility of which would be to enhance border enforcement operationally. The proposed entity was to be a merger of FEMA, the U.S. Customs Service, the U.S. Coast Guard, and the U.S. Border Patrol (a subordinate element of the Immigration and Naturalization Service (INS), as well as some offices within other agencies.[15] That proposal had, however, several notable shortcomings. First, it overlooked the fact that most immigration enforcement is conducted by INS inspectors – not by the Border Patrol, whose mission only involves the area *between* the fixed ports of entry into to the United States. The September 11 terrorists all entered the United States through fixed ports. Hart-Rudman also did not include in their proposed new entity other agencies with significant "border" responsibilities, including the U.S. Secret Service and other Department of Treasury enforcement authorities (for the international flow of illegal financial resources), the Department of Agriculture (for the illegal importation of agricultural commodities), or the Department of Health and Human Services (for international disease prevention and control). Perhaps most important, many of the agencies mentioned (especially the two entire agencies tagged by Hart-Rudman to move from their existing agencies – Customs and the Coast Guard) each have significant responsibilities beyond looking for terrorists. Customs has significant revenue collection responsibilities for imported goods – the primary reason for its existence. The Coast Guard has responsibility for marine safety and for marine search and rescue – two very significant missions.

Moreover, the intent of Hart-Rudman – "operationalizing" border enforcement more effectively – can be implemented without the Draconian approach of that proposal; and the Office of Homeland Security should have the authority to direct it and to ensure that appropriate resources are available for its implementation. The proposition is simple: create operational joint tasks forces with elements of those agencies with border responsibilities on an as-needed basis. Bring together those field operating elements of border agencies – where needed, in the right structure for the specific mission, for the required duration – to accomplish identified tasks. There is not merely historical precedent for such entities;[16] history has shown that, when field-operating personnel from various agencies are required to operate collectively, they usually find effective solutions to the problem at hand.

Clearly, Tom Ridge could seek a presidential decision to implement such an operational activity, but why should he need to do that? If the president needs to give his approval to every such undertaking, why not simply have a staff develop proposals for his consideration? It would not take someone of Tom Ridge's stature to do that.

CONCLUSION

It is obviously too soon to judge the effectiveness of the new Office of Homeland Security within the parameters of its existing authority. As long as the head of that office enjoys the full confidence and the backing of the president – and at any point in time everyone understands that – it may work very well. If the people or the relationships should change, then the results could be different. The activities of that office over time will likely indicate if additional authority is warranted. Congress is likely to watch the process very carefully and will, no doubt, step in at some point if members are not satisfied with the new structure and process.

ENDNOTES

1 Presidential Decision Directives 39 and 52

2 Colin Powell, Donald Rumsfeld, Tommy Thompson, John Ashcroft, and Joe Allbaugh each testified.

3 Statement by the president, "Domestic Preparedness Against Weapons of Mass Destruction," The White House, May 8, 2001.

4 Including the congressionally mandated National Commission on Terrorism, the Advisory Panel to Assess Domestic Response Capabilities for Terrorism Involving Weapons of Mass Destruction (also known as the "Gilmore Commission"), and the United States Commission on National Security/21st Century (also known as the "Hart-Rudman Commission"), as well as position papers from not-for-profit entities such as the Center for Strategic and International Studies (CSIS) and the Stimson Center

5 Executive Order Establishing Office of Homeland Security, The White House, October 8, 2001, available at http://www.whitehouse.gov.

6 In the summer of 1989, then-Secretary of Defense Dick Cheney declared that stemming the flow of illegal drugs into the United States "is a high priority national security mission" for the Department of Defense.

7 See that language in the discussion of "Authority Issues," below.

8 Executive Order Establishing Office of Homeland Security, Sec. 9.

9 Ibid., Sec. 2.

10 Ibid., Sec. 3.

11 "Facilitate" is used three times; "review," six.

12 21 U.S. Code, Sections 1701 et seq.

13 See, for example, H.R. 3026 (107th Congress, 1st Session, October 4, 2001), a bill "To establish an Office of Homeland Security within the Executive Office of the President to lead, oversee, and coordinate a comprehensive national homeland security strategy to safeguard the Nation," introduced by Representatives Gibbons, Harman, and others.

14 *ROAD MAP FOR NATIONAL SECURITY: Imperative for Change,* United States Commission on National Security/21st Century, March 15, 2001.

15 Ibid., pp. 13-20

16 The operational joint task forces formed in the late 1980s to combat the flow of illegal drugs across our southern borders.

TRANSFORMING BORDER MANAGEMENT IN THE POST-SEPTEMBER 11 WORLD

Stephen E. Flynn

A funny thing happened on the way towards globalization in the 1990s – as nations increasingly opened their borders to facilitate trade and travel, no one paid much attention to security. Looking back, discounting the security imperative appears to have been a bit like snubbing a teetotaler in making out invitations for a New Year's bash – we didn't want a bit of sobriety getting in the way of a good party. But the terrorist attacks on the World Trade Center and Pentagon and the subsequent anthrax mailings have become our bad morning after.

The tragic events of September 11 and our response to them have brought into stark relief one of the central paradoxes of the modern age. On the one hand, nations must remain open to the movement of people, goods, and ideas if they are to prosper. At the same time, openness without credible controls makes possible the rapid spread of a whole range of transnational threats including biohazards, contagious diseases, crime, and terrorism. As these problems proliferate, they create greater pressures on the state to play a more aggressive role in filtering the bad from the good. Historically, this sifting is done at national borders by stopping and examining the people, conveyances, and cargo at the port of entry. Accordingly, as the threat level rises, so too does the pressure on border management. In the extreme case of the 9-11 attacks, the United States effectively closed its borders by grounding aviation, stopping all vessel movements in its major ports, and reducing to a trickle the flow of people and vehicles entering the United States from Canada and Mexico.

So while the economic integrative imperative of globalization calls for borders to become increasingly porous, policymakers anxious about reigning in globalization's dark side look to the border to fend off contrabands, criminals, illegal migrants, and terrorists. The clash associated with this border dialectic – as a line that links versus one that separates – in our post-September world promises increasingly to be a messy one. But it also could and should be avoided. Developing the means to manage terrorist threats and other transnational muck that is contaminating the integrative process within the global community is essential, but we need to liberate ourselves from the notion that the border is the best place for accomplishing this. Indeed, an over reliance on the border to regulate and police the flow of goods and people can contribute to the problem.

Imagine this dark scenario. Suppose a terrorist loaded a chemical weapon in a freight container that is triggered by opening its door. He then has the container shipped from an overseas destination to an importer in the New York area. Now suppose an alert customs inspector working in the port of Newark deemed the container to be suspicious and decided to open it to inspect its contents, setting off the bomb. The effects would not be limited just to the maritime terminals within the East Coast's largest container port. The plume from a chemical weapon could readily contaminate the adjacent railroad tracks that link the northeast to the continental rail system, the New Jersey Turnpike, and the Newark International Airport – all of which are located within one mile of the container terminal. In addition to the loss of life, the economic consequences of cutting off the flow of cargo to a market of over 40 million consumers within a 200-mile radius are almost too painful to contemplate, but would certainly represent an important victory for the bad guys. The lesson: the port of entry is hardly an optimal place for detecting and intercepting a terrorist.

At the other end of the spectrum, consider the seemingly mundane case of Mexican trucking that garnered a good deal of public attention during the summer of 2001. The Teamsters Union undertook an aggressive public relations campaign to warn the American public and legislators on Capitol Hill of pending highway carnage if Mexican trucks were allowed to travel beyond a roughly 20-mile border commercial zone.[1] "Exhibit A" of the Teamsters case is a 36 percent safety inspection failure rate of Mexican trucks as reported in a May 2001 Federal Motor Carrier Safety Administration Inspector General's Report (the failure rate for U.S. trucks is 24 percent).[2] Presumably, Congress would be issuing a death sentence to innocent American motorists if it does not continue the U.S. ban on long-haul Mexican trucking, even in the face of a NAFTA arbitration panel's ruling that the ban violates the terms of the trade agreement.

But these statistics on inspection failures don't tell the real story. The reason that so many Mexican trucks operating at the border are old and poorly maintained is because it is uneconomical to run a state-of-the-art rig. Waiting hours at a border crossing in order to make a 20-mile round trip, with an empty trailer on the return, is not a lucrative business. Moving intercontinental freight is, so the trucks and drivers who make long-haul journeys tend to be of a higher quality. The situation is analogous to keeping an old jalopy for short runs to the corner store and using the well-maintained, newer car for the trip to visit out-of-state relatives. If the border were more open, there would be less need for these short, inefficient runs and much of the Mexican trucking inventory would be making one-way trips to the junkyard.

Next, there is the case of contraband smuggling. The White House Office of National Drug Control Policy estimates that more than half of the cocaine that arrives in the United States comes via the southwest border.[3] This should come as no surprise, since there are so many places to hide given the growing volume of vehicles, trucks, and railcars that enter the United States each day. In Laredo, for instance, truck crossings have risen 116 percent, from 1.3 million in 1993 to 2.8 million in 1999. Passenger vehicles have increased from 14.1 million to 17.1 million over the same time period.[4] Faced with these volumes, the U.S. Customs Service is charged with monitoring compliance with more than 400 laws and 34 international treaties, statutes, agreements, and conventions on behalf of 40 federal agencies – but it must do this while being mindful of the need to facilitate the flow of legitimate trade and travelers.[5] Despite the rising number of inspectors and investigators assigned to the 28 border-entry points in Texas, New Mexico, Arizona, and California, the service is facing "needle-in-a-haystack" odds as it strives to detect and intercept illicit drugs. That analogy is no exaggeration given that the pure cocaine to feed America's annual coke habit could be transported in just 15 40-foot containers and that it takes on average five agents three hours to thoroughly inspect a single 40-foot container.[6]

When the vulnerability of the trucking sector that services the border zone is combined with the mounting pressures on customs and immigration inspectors to minimize any disruption to legitimate commerce, the results are nearly ideal conditions for smuggling. Not only are short-haul rigs more likely to be unsafe, but they are also easy marks for traffickers keen to get a load of narcotics across the border. This is because the drivers of these rigs tend to be younger, less skilled, and are paid only nominal wages – as little as $7 to $10 per trip – as compared to drivers of long-haul rigs. As a result, the potential payoff for carrying drugs through a congested border crossing is all the more tempting. Also, there is ample time and opportunity within a Mexican and U.S. border city for these illicit transfers to occur between the forwarder facility where the short-haul rig picks up a load, and the border where it is likely to receive only a cursory examination by a hopelessly overworked customs inspector.

Then there is the issue of illegal migration. Stepped-up patrolling and policing of the border may raise the costs of getting to the United States, but it also creates a demand for those who are in the business of arranging the illegal crossings. As the "coyote" business becomes more lucrative, criminal gangs are better positioned to invest in pay-offs and put together increasingly sophisticated smuggling operations.[7] Again, as with narcotics, there are ample opportunities for hiding illegal migrants among the growing tide of truck and vehicle traffic moving through congested ports of entry.

In short, the prevalence along the border of organized criminal activity, unsafe trucks, and drivers who are not likely to quibble over distinctions between legal and illegal cargo, has a good deal to do with the chaotic nature of living life in the border slow-lane. The combined forces of burgeoning cross-border traffic, severe infrastructure constraints, and, ironically, added delays that result from stepped-up efforts to detect and intercept illicit activities at the border is making the border more difficult to police. This unintended consequence has sobering security implications in the context of the September 11 attacks, since they create fertile conditions for terrorists to exploit.

Thus, we face something of a border control paradox: rising crime and security risks lead policymakers to hardened borders, but the chaotic environment associated with hardened borders can be a boon for criminals and terrorists. Is there any way around this conundrum? There is, if we are willing to look beyond the border as the locus for securing public safety and security.

A stepping-off point is to reign in the homeland security rhetoric that proclaims the need to do more to "protect" the nation's borders – nobody in Canada or Mexico is trying to steal them! America's vital interests are not tied to defending a line in the sand to the south or among the trees to the north, but to advancing greater regional and global market integration while managing important safety, security, and other public policy interests. This balancing act can be accomplished by: (1) developing the means to validate in advance the overwhelming majority of the people and goods that cross the border as law-abiding and low-risk; and (2) enhancing the means for agents to target and intercept inbound high-risk people and goods away from the border. Accomplishing the first is key to succeeding at the second, since there will always be limits on the time and resources available for agents to conduct investigations and inspections. The goal must be to limit the size of the haystack in which there are most likely to be illicit and dangerous needles.

Verifying legitimate cross-border flows as truly legitimate is not as fearsome task as it might first appear. The aggregate numbers suggest that border control agents are facing impossible odds. Legal entry into the United States is authorized at 3,700 terminals in 301 ports of entry. In 2000 alone, approximately 489 million people, 128 million passenger vehicles, 11 million maritime containers, 11.5 million trucks, 2.2 million railroad cars, 964,000 planes, and 211,000 vessels passed through U.S. border inspection systems.[8] And the majority of this traffic was concentrated in just a handful of ports and border crossings. One third of all the trucks that enter the United States annually, for example, traverse just four international bridges between the province of Ontario and the states of Michigan and New York.[9] In fact, more trade flowed on the back of trucks crossing just one bridge between Windsor, Ontario, and Detroit, Michigan, than the United States conducts with all of China.[10]

The aggregate border-crossing numbers can be misleading, however, since so many of the vehicles, drivers, and people are regular customers. For instance, while there were 4.2 million recorded truck crossings on the southwest border in 1999, these crossings were made by roughly 80,000 trucks.[11] Of the more than 350,000 U.S. importers, the top 1,000 companies are responsible for approximately 60 percent of all goods by value.[12] The top 100 imported 35 percent.[13] And many of the more than 130,000 people that pass each day through the San Yisdro border crossing are Mexican workers commuting to their job in San Diego.[14]

Since the overwhelming majority of people, conveyances, and cargo are both legitimate and familiar, the border management function would be well served by developing the means to reliably validate its legal identity and purpose. In so doing, two things can be accomplished. First, it will be easier to identify with confidence travelers or goods that are, in fact, low-risk. Second, when regulatory and enforcement agents have intelligence that a person or good may be compromised, they can target their detection and interception efforts with greater precision.

To confirm the legal identity and purpose of international travelers, off-the-shelf technologies could be readily embraced to move away from easily forgeable paper-based documents such as traditional visas or passports. Governments could embrace universal biometric travel identification cards that would contain electronically scanned fingerprints or retina or iris information. These ATM-style cards would be issued by consulates and passport offices and presented at the originating and connecting points of an individual's international travel itinerary. Airports, rail stations, rental car agencies, and bus terminals would all be required to install and operate card readers for any customers moving across national jurisdictions. Once entered, electronic identity information would be forwarded in real time to the jurisdiction of the final destination. The objective would be to provide authorities with the opportunity to check the identity information against their watch lists. If no red flags appeared, it would not be necessary to conduct a time-consuming and intrusive search. For noncitizens, a country could require the presentation of these cards for renting cars, flying on domestic flights, or using passenger rail service.

Confirming in advance that the contents of a freight container are what they are advertised to be is a daunting task, but it is a doable one. Worldwide, several million companies are in the business of moving goods and loading more than 50 million containers,[15] sealing them with a numbered plastic seal, and sending them around the planet. At present, there are no standards governing who and what loads these containers, so every one is essentially a mystery box until it is opened and its contents inspected. They don't have to be mysteries.

The international community should establish standards that mandate that containers be loaded in an approved, security-sanitized facility. These facilities would have loading docks secured from unauthorized entry and the loading process monitored by camera. In high-risk areas, the use of cargo and vehicle scanners might be required, with the images stored so that they can be cross-checked with images taken by inspectors at a transshipment or arrival destination.

After loading, containers would have to be fitted with theft-resistant mechanical and electronic seals. As added assurance against tampering once the container is on the move, a light or temperature sensor could be installed in the interior, programmed to set off an alarm if the container were opened illegally at some point during transit. The drivers of the trucks that deliver goods to the port would be subjected to mandatory background checks and issued biometrically based identity cards. The routes of trucks from the factory to the ports of embarkation could be monitored by GPS transponders attached to the cab, chassis, and container. The transponder, like those used for the "E-Z-pass" toll-payment system across the northeastern United States, would give authorities the ability to monitor each vehicle's movements, and it would be programmed so that tampering with it would result in an automatic alert to the police. Importers and shippers could be required to make this tracking information available upon request to regulatory or enforcement authorities within the jurisdictions through which it would be destined.

Manufacturers, importers, shipping companies, and commercial carriers, finally, could agree to provide to the authorities, with advance notice, the details about their shipments, operators, and conveyances. This early notice would give inspectors the time to assess the validity of the data, check it against any watch lists they may be maintaining, and provide support to a field inspector deciding what should be targeted for examination. This information-sharing, when combined with the requirement for real-time tracking of truck movements, should deter and help to detect any effort to intercept and compromise the integrity of the shipments from the factor until they arrive at their destination.

As with many safety or universal quality control standards, private trade associations could hold much of the responsibility for monitoring compliance with these security measures. As a condition of joining and maintaining membership within an association, a company would be subjected to a preliminary review of their security measures and would agree to submit to periodic and random spot checks. Without membership, access to ships servicing the mega-ports, in turn, would be denied.

While the private sector may be tempted to balk at these requirements, they are not, in fact, radical impositions. For most modern firms, it is in their own interest to invest in the kinds of systems that provide greater levels of oversight and control throughout the international transportation process. This is because their profitability is tied in no small part to their ability to satisfy growing competitive pressures to embrace supply-chain management imperatives built around efforts to trim inventories, execute increasingly short product-cycles, and to meet "just-in-time" delivery schedules. Prospering in the global marketplace increasingly requires constructing virtual worldwide assembly lines with minimally stocked shelves which, in term, makes compulsory a degree of logistical choreography impossible just a few years ago. Given the high costs associated with cargo losses or delays, managers want guarantees that goods will arrive by the date specified in the contract. Many transportation and logistics firms are responding by embracing new tagging, tracking, communications, and information technologies that make it possible to monitor in near real time the flow of products and passengers as they move from their points of origin to their final destinations. Shipper Web sites, such as those developed by the Ohio-based Roadway Express, provide customers with their own personal home page where they can monitor all their active shipments aboard the company's global positioning system-equipped trucking fleet, including their current locations and a constantly updated estimate of the expected delivery times.[16]

Security concerns are also receiving new priority in the global marketplace, since the importance of guaranteeing delivery has placed a premium on tightening safeguards within the transportation industry. According to the National Cargo Security Council, American companies lose an estimated $12 to $15 billion a year in stolen cargo.[17] The computer industry has been particularly hard hit, with theft and insurance costs adding an estimated 10 percent to the cost of the average personal computer. Sixty high-tech companies with combined annual revenues of $750 billion have responded by forming the Technology Asset Protection Association (TAPA). Founded in 1997, TAPA has identified a comprehensive set of security practices to govern the shipment of members' supplies and products. If a freight forwarder or carrier wants to do business with any of TAPA's well-heeled members, they must adopt these practices.[18]

Thus market pressures are mounting for participants in the transportation and logistics industries to embrace standards and adopt processes that can make many border-control activities redundant or irrelevant. In response to these pressures, companies are becoming better able to implement safeguards, police themselves, and provide useful and timely information necessary for public security – information that inspectors have traditionally tried to verify independently at border crossings. Theft-resistant transportation networks are more difficult for criminals and terrorists to compromise. Should there be advance intelligence of such a compromise, these information systems will make it easier to locate and interdict a contaminated shipment before it enters a crowded port; alternatively, authorities can put together a "controlled-delivery" sting operation, where the contraband is allowed to reach the intended recipient so that the appropriate arrests can be made.

The U.S. government could provide further incentives for these kinds of investments by making new investments in transportation infrastructure at and near the border with intelligent transportation system (ITS) technologies built into that infrastructure. Specifically, the Transportation Equity Act for the 21st Century has targeted substantial funding for major roadway improvements under the Coordinated Border Infrastructure Program.[19] As development and management plans for such projects as the "Ports-to-Plain" Corridor and the I-69 NAFTA highway are drawn-up, a "smart dedicated trade lane" could be incorporated into its design. That is, like commuter "High Occupancy Vehicle" (HOV) lanes found around many metropolitan areas, access to a dedicated trade lane would be restricted to only those vehicles and drivers and that cargo that participates in the new border management regime.

An additional incentive could come by moving many of the border entry inspection processes away from the physical border itself and instead consolidating them into a single trilateral "NAFTA inspection facility," located on a dedicated traffic lane that leads to the border. For instance there is an 18-mile new toll road leading from I-39 to the Mexican state of Nueva Leon via the recently constructed Colombia Bridge on the outskirts of Laredo, Texas. Northbound trucks from Mexico City and Monterey and southbound trucks headed toward the Mexican interior would have to stop just once at a location where there is plenty of space to conduct inspections, so there is no risk of hours-long back-ups that now routinely plague the bridges. Once the trucks are cleared, the flow of traffic could be closely monitored by use of "intelligent transportation systems" (ITS) technologies. In the case of maritime shipments, inspectors could work side-by-side in ports such as Halifax, Vancouver, Long Beach, Miami, or Newark, examining goods destined for their jurisdictions.

But simply relocating where inspections take place is not enough. Border control agencies need to fundamentally change the way they are doing business as well. The days of random, tedious, paperbound, labor-intensive border inspection systems – the bane of every legitimate international traveler and business – should be numbered. The manpower constraints inherent in traditional border-control practices guarantee their continuing inability to adequately police the surge in NAFTA commerce. What is the alternative? The answer lies in a relatively new concept being developed by cyber-security experts, known as "anomaly detection."

In the computer industry, "anomaly detection" represents the most promising means for detecting hackers intent on stealing data or transmitting computer viruses.[20] The process involves monitoring the cascading flows of computer traffic with an eye towards discerning what is "normal" traffic; i.e., that which moves by way of the most techno-logically rational route. Once this baseline is established, software is written to detect that which is aberrant. A good computer hacker will try to look as close as possible to a legitimate user. But, since he is not, he inevitably must do some things differently, and good cyber-security software will detect that variation, and deny access. For those hackers who manage to get through, their breach is identified and shared so that this abnormal behavior can be removed from the guidance of what is "normal" and acceptable.

In much the same way, the overwhelming majority of the vehicles, people, and cargo that move through international transportation networks move in predictable patterns. If we have the means to analyze and keep track of these flows, we will have the means to detect "aberrant" behavior such as high-valued goods being shipped on slow conveyances via circuitous routes. In short, "anomaly detection" of cross-border flows is possible if the regulatory and enforcement agencies whose daily tasks are to police those flows: (1) are given access to intelligence about real or suspected threats, and (2) are provided the means to gather, share, and mine private-sector data that provides a comprehensive picture of "normal" cross-border traffic so as to enhance their odds of detecting threats when they materialize.

If the public sector undertakes these changes, the private sector must also change its attitude about engaging in self-policing and sharing anything but the minimum amounts of relevant data with government agencies. As the events of September 11 have certainly made clear, border control agencies have important and legitimate jobs to perform. And it is not just the terrorist threat that mandates that there be better controls within the global flows of people and good. The general public wants restrictions on the flows of contraband such as weapons, drugs, and child pornography. Immigration policies require that who enters and who leaves their jurisdictions be monitored and controlled. Many public-health strategies aimed at managing the spread of disease require the identification and isolation of people, livestock, and agricultural products that could place the general population at risk. Safety and environmental threats connected with unsafe shipping and trucking mandate that the transportation sector be monitored. And trade rules must be enforced for trade agreements to be sustainable.

While these process changes hold out the prospect of dramatically improving both the security within and facilitation of legitimate trade and travel, there remain important bureaucratic impediments among U.S. border control agencies in achieving them. While the stakes associated with getting border management right are enormous, there is no one ultimately in charge of accomplishing it. Responsibility for inspecting cargo is split among the U.S. Customs Service that is a part of the Department of Treasury; the Food and Drug Administration (FDA) and agricultural inspectors that belong to the Department of Agriculture; and, for hazardous materials, the Environmental Protection Agency (EPA), which is an independent agency. Responsibility for inspecting people at the ports of entry is the task of the Immigration and Naturalization Service (INS), which is an agency within the Department of Justice. The U.S. Coast Guard is responsible for inspecting ships and securing ports. Its commandant reports to the Secretary of Transportation.

The front-line inspectors for all these border control agencies desperately need communication and decision-support tools to carry out their jobs. The data-management systems that support their work are old and frail computer mainframes. While it may be technologically feasible to upgrade these systems so that agencies could share information among one another, currently there are legal firewalls that make it difficult or impossible to do so. The problem could be made more manageable if existing data collection requirements were examined with an eye towards identifying what should be eliminated, consolidated, or accomplished by other methods such as statistical sampling. The goal should be to create one clearinghouse for receiving data about people, cargo, and conveyances. All government agency users of the data could then collect and analyze what they needed from that pool.

Inspectors and investigators assigned to border control agencies will continue to play a critical role in the timely detection and interception of anomalies. To be effective, however, a serious effort must be made to improve their pay, staffing numbers, and training, and to push them beyond the border itself into common bilateral or multilateral international inspection zones. Megaports and regional transshipment ports should play host to these zones and allow agents from a number of countries to work side-by-side. Such an approach would take better advantage of information collected by law enforcement officials at the point of departure, allow transport-related intelligence to get into the security system sooner, and reduce the congestion caused by concentrating all inspections at the final destination. The bilateral inspection zones set up by French and British officials at both ends of the English Channel tunnel could serve as a model.

Fundamentally transforming border management will certainly be costly in terms of resources, bureaucratic angst, and political capital. But, the costs of not making changes are greater. In light of the events of September 11, it would be irresponsible for the U.S. government not to attend to the vulnerabilities associated with trade and travel networks so open that they practically invite terrorists to do their worst. What we witnessed on September 11 is how warfare will be conducted in the 21st century. U.S. conventional military dominance, ironically, has made the world safe for asymmetric warfare. The lethal precision U.S. forces displayed in the Persian Gulf War, over the Balkan skies, and more recently in Afghanistan have made one thing clear: any attempt to enjoin the United States on the conventional field of battle promises to be a losing proposition. So America's adversaries will likely opt for unconventional attacks that can produce the kind of social and economic disruption achieved by the strikes on the World Trade Center and the anthrax mailings.

And the United States will have adversaries who will find irresistible the appeal of catastrophic terrorism. This is true regardless of what happens to Osama bin Laden and the al Qaeda network. America's cultural, economic, and military dominance makes it public enemy No. 1 for any nation or group unhappy with the global status quo. Those who are inclined to give form to their anti-American angst will look to exploit the openness of our civil and economic lives. This is not simply to kill Americans and destroy our landmarks. The aim is to spawn a reaction – or overreaction – that chips away at the foundation of American power and prosperity: our freedoms and global reach.

Focusing on point-of-origin security measures and embracing the use of new technologies support the homeland security mission by enhancing the ability of front-line agencies to detect and intercept global terrorist activity before it can arrive on U.S. soil. This approach also precludes the need to impose draconian measures in response to the terrorist threat along our national borders and within our airports and seaport that has the effect of imposing a self-embargo on the American economy. It will require providing meaningful incentives to companies and travelers to win over their support. It mandates a serious infusion of resources to train and equip front-line border control agencies to operate and collaborate in this more complex trade and security environment. And it involves mobilizing U.S. allies and trade partners to harmonize these processes throughout the global transportation networks.

Building a credible system for detecting and intercepting terrorists who seek to exploit or target international transport networks would go a long way towards containing the disruption potential of a catastrophic terrorist act. Ultimately, getting border management right must not be about fortifying our nation at the water's and land's edge to fend off terrorists. Instead, its aim must be to identify and take the necessary steps to preserve the flow of trade and travel that allows the United States to remain the open, prosperous, free, and globally engaged societies that rightly inspires so many in this shrinking and dangerous world.

ENDNOTES

1 International Brotherhood of Teamsters, *Teamsters News Press Release*: "Hoffa Warns Senate Committee of Perils in Admitting Unsafe Mexican Trucks" (July 19, 2001).

2 Office of the Inspector General, Interim Report on Status of Implementing the North American Free Trade Agreement's Cross-Border Trucking Provisions, Federal Motor Carrier Safety Administration, MH-2001-059, (May 8, 2001): 7.

3 Office of National Drug Control Policy, *The National Drug Control Strategy: 2001 Annual Report, Shielding U.S. Borders from the Drug Threat* (Washington: USGPO, 2001).

4 Philips, K. and C. Manzanares. "Transportation Infrastructure and the Border Economy," *The Border Economy*, (Dallas, TX: Federal Reserve Bank of Dallas, June 2001): 11.

5 http://www.customs.gov/about/about.htm

6 See Stephen E. Flynn, "Beyond Border Control," *Foreign Affairs,* Volume 79, No. 6, (Nov/Dec. 2000) p. 59.

7 Andreas, P. *Border Games: Policing the U.S.-Mexico Divide*, (Ithaca: Cornell Univ. Press, 2000).

8 Figures on truck, train, and passenger vehicle crossings provided by the Bureau of Transportation Statistics. People, vessel, and plane statistics are based on FY00 CLEAR and OMR Data as displayed at www.customs.gov/about/about.htm. Container statistic provided by MARAD, Office of Statistical & Economic Analysis.

9 Transport Canada, Transportation in Canada 2000 Annual Report, p. 88 (Table 10-7: Twenty Largest Border Crossings for Trucks, 1998-1999)

10 Based on U.S. Census and figures provided by the Detroit International Bridge Company.

11 Office of the Inspector General, Interim Report on Status of Implementing the North American Free Trade Agreement's Cross Border Trucking Provisions, Federal Motor Carrier Safety Administration, MH-2001-059, (May 8, 2001): 7. Also, Statement of the Honorable Kenneth M. Mead, Inspector General, USDOT, "Motor Carrier Safety at the U.S.–Mexican Border," July 18, 2001 before the Committee on Commerce, Science, and Transportation, United States

Senate.

12 U.S. Customs Service, *Trade Compliance & Enforcement Plan.*

13 Remarks by Kathleen Haage, Area Director New York-New Jersey, U.S. Customs Service at Barthco Briefing on "Trade Partnerships Against Terrorism," January 23, 2002.

14 Jessica Baker, Regional Planning in San Diego and Tijuana, *An Interview with Nan Valerio, Senior Planner for the San Diego Association of Governments,* 2001.

15 United Nations Conference on Trade and Development, *Review of Maritime Transport 2000*, p. 49.

16 http://www.roadway.com

17 Telephone interview with Joseph Baker, Executive Director, National Cargo Security Council, Washington, D.C., August 2001.

18 http://www.tapa3.org/

19 TEA-21 [1119(a)]

20 http://www.cerias.purdue.edu/coast/ids/ids-body.html

INTERDEPENDENCE, GLOBALIZATION, AND NORTH AMERICAN BORDERS

George Haynal

PREFACE

This paper is a discussion of the Canada/U.S. border and its role in the protection of national security. It is argued here that the relationship between security and the border is more tenuous than had generally been acknowledged before the events of September 11.

The border, as it is now constituted, provides inadequate protection to either country against global threats to its security. Its main effect at this point is to protect each society against the real and perceived imperfections of the other. Given the high level of compatibility and growing economic integration between them, this role falls short of an objective that would justify the costs. Those costs, direct and indirect, are considerable. With an excessive mix of functions, under-resourced institutions and stressed infrastructure, the border is a source of risk to the smooth movement of flows on which the prosperity of both countries now depends.

The paper suggests that the concept of physical, earth-bound borders needs to be updated in the age of globalization. The threats to our countries in North America come largely from *outside* our territories. The border we erect to defend ourselves must address the reality that these external threats come from "everywhere and nowhere" in physical space, from borderless networks empowered by technology.

The paper proposes that our governments:

1. Commit, at the highest possible level, to the creation of an "Area of Mutual Confidence" for the protection of security in North America, and in the spirit of that commitment:

2. Continue to intensify action within, and cooperation across, their jurisdictions to address global security threats,

3. Expand this bilateral cooperation on to the multilateral level, and

4. Establish a shared, high-level institution to help guide binational approaches to borders.

This paper is focused on the Canada/U.S. border. There is no question, however, that Mexico's border with the United States provides unique challenges that also need to be addressed. There is also no question that any approach developed on the Canada/U.S. border would need, in time, to be adapted to that on the south. The same dynamic of economic integration that unites Canada and the United States also joins them to Mexico. The level of comity between Canada and the United States, however, is not yet matched in the south. Every effort must be expended to ensure that it is, and that Mexico is able to participate fully as soon as possible in a North America area of mutual confidence to defend our continent against global threats.

THE PRESENT DISCOURSE ON BORDERS

Post September 11

One of the first actions of the U.S. authorities on September 11 was to seal the northern border (along with every other). This reaction was a natural component of its response to external attack, though it seems to have added little to the country's security and stranded many U.S. travelers in Canada (where the population demonstrated a characteristic and spontaneous openness). The move did have a useful didactic effect. With the border first sealed and then "working to rule," the interdependence of the two societies became brutally clear. Daily merchandise trade worth $1.5 billion was jeopardized, as was the passage of an average of .6 million people who cross the border daily. Uncertainty about the seamlessness of the border raised concerns in Canada about the viability of the Canadian economy. "Just in Time" manufacturing was suddenly seen as vulnerable. Governments worried about perception of additional "country risk" among investors. Other issues that had not yet earned a place in the national discourse suddenly loomed large on the public agenda, including the concern that Canada's own defenses were inadequate.

A more limited discourse on border issues developed in the United States. At first, it focused on the perception that the northern border had become a point of vulnerability. It was only gradually that the close nature of cross-border relations and the economic importance of a smoothly operating border with the country's most important trading partner came into the picture.

Pre September 11

The bi-national wake-up call was an important breakthrough (and, may provide a moment of opportunity to get the border right). It has already energized efforts by the two national governments to bring the shared or "inner" border between Canada and the United States up to date. Various agency-to-agency initiatives were already pursuing this objective (The Border Vision, the Cross Border Crime Forum, the Border Accord) and were making progress. Nonetheless, resource constraints, and the lack of national priority attached to these efforts, kept change within narrow limits.

In 1999, as a way to engage a broader constituency and to foster a national discourse, the prime minister and the president mandated a broad process of consultation labeled the "Canada U.S. Partnership" (CUSP). The process was intended to produce a new vision of a border that was appropriate to the 21st century. CUSP did produce an interim report of some interest, drawing on the views of stakeholders at two major consultations.[1] The report stressed the imperative of a balanced approach to border management with a view to both providing security and facilitating the seamless passage virtuous flows essential to both countries. It was the intention of the two governments to carry forward this consultation with stakeholders and thus establish a bi-national consensus in favor of more far-reaching changes in border management. Then, September 11 intervened, and the process of reinventing the border assumed an unprecedented urgency. It will be no less challenging now than before September 11, but the basic problem, at least, is better understood: the very notion of a traditional land border between Canada and the United States needs to be updated.

TRADITIONAL BORDERS ARE OUTDATED, BUT THEIR VALUE IS CONTROVERSIAL

Global flows, both constructive and threatening, increasingly treat borders as irrelevant. Though citizens in both our countries value the inner border, neither Canadian nor U.S. society feels constrained by it. Quite the contrary, integration between the two economies is posited on the implicit notion that the border would become ever less a factor. More generally, physical borders that are maintained separately by individual jurisdictions are increasingly redundant in the context of a global economy, the growth of a global community of values and the increase of commerce in virtual space.

Questions about the purposes of the Canada/U.S. border as presently conceived are particularly clear in the minds of economic decision-makers. They see the border's role largely in the context of North American economic integration and contrast it with the success of a more intense process of regional community building in Europe, which has resulted in the virtual elimination of internal borders.

Public perception in our countries is, however, more complex, and shows a high level of attachment to the border. While many are ready for change, many see the present border as an important symbol and effective guarantor of sovereignty. Those, particularly in Canada, who are concerned about reform of the "inner" border often see such an effort as a proxy for diminishing Canada's sovereignty. They are worried about the loss of a capacity for independent action in economic and social policy, in the adjudication of individual and collective rights, in the allocations of public goods. Thus, the debate about reform of the Canada/U.S. border needs, at some point, to engage in issues that have little to do directly with the border itself, but about the policy space behind it. The scope of this paper is restricted to the border's security purposes, but even in that area, there is a tension to be resolved between the desire to ensure sovereignty on the one hand and expectations for seamlessness on the other. That tension was building before September

11. Now, it is unavoidable, and demands action. Its resolution will be among the defining policy challenges to the two governments over the coming years. It will demand agreement on a broader approach to security and about the nature of borders in general, including those that face outward.

THE BORDER: A SHORT HISTORY

It might be useful, as we contemplate its future, to recall how closely the Canada/U.S. border's long history has tracked the evolution of a relationship between our societies from savage hostility to intimate friendship.

The colonial powers began to map out their claims to North American territory in the 16th century. The fact that those claims often overlapped had marginal practical meaning until well over a century later when the new world became a peripheral front in broader European war. Control (often theoretical) over vast territories and power over increasing numbers of (real) North Americans was traded repeatedly. The conflicts in North America may have been a sideshow for Europe, but there were real economic and physical security issues at stake in where the boundaries were drawn for those on the ground. Access to fur trade routes and guarantees of physical security for colonists were at the heart of cross-border disputes as then waged by British, French, and Aboriginal protagonists. Terrorism of the most lurid kind was part of the arsenal employed in this intra North American conflict, as was what we would now label "ethnic cleansing" as borders were drawn and redrawn throughout the 17th and 18th centuries.

The border continued to be characterized by conflict after the American Revolution created two polities out of British North America. Land invasions were a feature of the Revolutionary War and resumed again in the early 19th century. Former Americans fought alongside former French colonists to maintain Canada under the British Crown. Over the next decades public opinion gradually came to terms with the notion that what had been British North America would remain permanently divided. Cross border raids by dissenters, however, persisted well through the 19th century.[2] The Civil War and its after effects had a dramatic impact on the relationship and the border. Quixotic Confederate schemes to invade the Union from Canada and a view that Britain had supported the Confederacy led the United States to abandon the form of free trade established under the Reciprocity Treaty of June 1854. (A demand for passports for Canadians to enter the United States was put into effect earlier.)[3]

Once the new Dominion was established, however, the United States acted against those who sought to invade Canada. It would henceforth never countenance military action against its northern neighbor (an approach gratefully reciprocated). Though progress was far from smooth, the security role of the border, in short, evolved dramatically and for the better throughout the 19th century.

By the beginning of the last century, the basis of the present-day relationship was firmly established, with the settlement of the last major border dispute over the B.C./Alaska border (an imperial betrayal in Canadian eyes) and the expressed desire in both countries to formalize cross border cooperation. That desire was driven in Canada's case in large part by a desire to assert its sovereignty and interests, independent of Great Britain.

The establishment of the International Joint Commission and other border arrangements signaled the beginning of this new, shared approach. "Good neighborliness" developed, despite the hiccup of Prohibition, into a value shared by both societies – a pride in having between them "the longest undefended border in the world."

President Roosevelt and Prime Minster Mackenzie King made the first commitment to a shared defense against external threats. They advanced the notion of North American "space," when, in 1940, at Ogdensburg (well before the United States entered World War II), they committed the two countries to mutual defense.

The post-war era saw further advances in both border and security cooperation, including in the foundation of NORAD for continental air defense. Free passage for people across the border was the norm (facilitated by the introduction of measures like air pre clearance in the 1970s), despite the controls that remained on the passage of goods.

All this is to say that the border has been a living expression of the broader relationship. Arguments for the immutability of the border ignore history. Border management has evolved to become a comfortable (perhaps complacent) and often informal partnership. Changes in the environment demand that this partnership move now to a new level.

THE BORDER TODAY

The Canada/U.S. border today is a jumble of contradictions. The publics in our two societies retain apparently conflicting sentiments about it. They expect it to pose no impediment to their movements, but they also treat it as an essential attribute of sovereignty, necessary for the protection of national security and the integrity of national institutions.

Despite free trade, the border still fulfills an accretion of responsibilities that, it can be argued, are often redundant and inappropriately restrictive. The CCRA administers over 180 legislative instruments on the border, many of which protect duplicative regulatory systems with identical or at the least, compatible objectives. Trade-restricting policies (e.g. those relating to rules of origin) are also applied at the border.

Governments had, until recently, largely neglected border reform as a strategic priority. They did so, it should be said in their defense, in a spirit of realism as well as expediency. They had a clear sense of the limits on what even a well-tended border could do, given geography. More important, they were acutely aware of the difficulties implicit in trying for real change, given contradictory public expectations and bureaucratic inertia. Nonetheless it was clear to both governments, even before September 11, that the persisting mismatch in the purposes and capacities at the border was becoming expensive and risky. They were moving, carefully, to fix it. What were the risks that governments saw?

THE BORDER CHALLENGED BY ECONOMIC INTEGRATION AND A GLOBALIZED WORLD: KEEP UP WITH GROWING VOLUME OF NORTH/SOUTH FLOWS... OR GET OUT OF THE WAY

Though the two countries have historically been important trading partners, the FTA has had a revolutionary impact on the level of mutual trading dependence. Volumes of flows have been growing exponentially since 1988. Over 40 percent of Canadian GDP is now accounted for by exports to or through the United States. Ensuring that those flows move unimpeded is a matter of survival for the Canadian economy. Given the differences in size and of their dependence on external trade, the importance of unimpeded access to Canadian markets is much less talked about in the United States. Only 2 percent of U.S. GDP is accounted for by exports to Canada, though Canada is the first export market for 38

U.S. states, and is critical to some. Canada, is, it needs to be repeated, the United States's most important trading partner (with Mexico, its other land neighbor, following quickly behind). It is also the locus for U.S. foreign investment of the first order, and is its most critical and diverse external source of natural resources.

Whatever the differences in the intensity of interdependence, the fact that the border was not keeping up with growth in traffic has been a growing source of concern in both countries, the more so since impairment of its capacity is, at least partly self inflicted. The bulk of Canada/U.S. traffic moves by road, and crosses at seven points. Most of the goods crossing the border do so free of duties or quantitative restrictions, subject to health and safety regulations that are as effective on one side of the border as on the other. Yet all these shipments are subject to the same levels of verification. Effective risk management requires a different approach. As the CUSP report observed, over 99 percent of flows are compliant. Efforts to focus in on the less than 1 percent that is not need to be accelerated if the border is to continue serve a useful purpose in risk management. The CCRA's Custom Blueprint has initiated important changes in this direction. The Smart Borders agreement concluded last month promises further, bilateral movement.

Investment in additional infrastructure at approaches to the border and at the actual crossing points will also be essential to accommodate what are certain to be growing volumes of cross-border traffic as economic integration proceeds. The most recent Canadian budget has assigned funding for this purpose on a scale out of keeping with any that has been available before. In the United States, T-21 funds are available. State and provincial commitments will need to be part of the mix.

More dramatic improvement is possible on both fronts. What it requires is sustained political attention even once the immediate anxieties raised by September 11 have passed. This will be the more important because meaningful change will also need to involve a reassessment of what responsibilities the border now fulfills, and of the differences in social and economic policy that it is meant to safeguard. But making the border more efficient will address only part of the problem. Traditional borders are less and less capable of providing security from global threats.

COPING WITH EXTERNAL THREATS

Information Technology Circumvents Borders

Borders exist to control the movement of people and of physical goods. They continue to perform that role, but now, advances in information technology make it possible for significant flows to circumvent the physical border altogether. Flows of benign information – news, culture, capital, scientific data, non-governmental networking – as well as virulent information – illicit funds, propaganda, terrorist networking – cross borders in virtual form. The view that physical borders can impede these growing flows is manifestly outdated.

A useful demonstration of how limited our own border is in such an environment was provided by the case of *Sports Illustrated*. That magazine, like all other foreign publications, had been prevented from publishing a split-run edition in Canada by virtue of legislation passed in the 1970s. In 1996, *Sports Illustrated* decided to defy this prohibition by the simple expedient of beaming it across the border for subsequent printing within the country. Special legislation, relating not to the border but to tax treatment of advertising and postal rates, had to be introduced to counter this move.

This relatively minor instance is perhaps out of context here. It does, however, serve to demonstrate the point: borders, (particularly the border between two countries so closely bound by virtual as well as physical flows as Canada and the United States) cannot any longer serve to protect national space from electronic penetration, even of the most innocuous kind. The only way that this "virtual" challenge can be addressed is in its own medium. "Virtual borders" need to be created for this purpose through a mix of domestic legislation, regulation, and policing, as well as networking on a global basis, all based in the deployment of sophisticated technology.

Physical Borders, Alone, Are Powerless to Control Virulent Physical Flows in a Globalized World

Similarly, new approaches, which place less stress on the physical border between Canada and the United States, are also demanded by global traffic in arms, drugs, people, capital, and hazardous goods. These flows are the domain of sophisticated criminal organizations operating on a global basis; they are aimed at both the United States and Canada (among other societies whose openness and affluence provides markets).

The border that separates our own two polities can only serve as an incidental line of defense against these offshore flows. Once they have reached this inner border, they have already succeeded in penetrating a largely integrated space. Even reinforcing our external physical borders at ports and airports that provide entry to North America would in of itself be insufficient, given the volumes of such virulent flows, the ease with which these flows can be hidden within the vast volumes of legitimate global trade, and the sophistication with which criminals organize globally. Fighting such flows also demands the construction of global and "virtual" borders, consisting of action within national jurisdictions, partnership between neighbors, and multilateral cooperation.

Adding National Security to the Mix of Objectives to Be Served on the Inner Border

Pressures for border reform were already in conflict before September 11: the first, to protect our joint economic security by ensuring that the border was as seamless as possible and offered the least possible impediment to the growing flows that were both the foundation of North American prosperity and critical to our identity as open societies, and the second, to protect "human security" by ensuring the best possible controls to impede "vicious" flows of drugs, trafficked people, arms, hazardous goods, hate propaganda, and the circulation of laundered money within North America.

The issue of "national security" as such, did not meaningfully enter the border mix[4] until the arrest of the Millennium bomber, an illegal resident of Canada at the border in December 1999. The frustration of that terrorist plot was a signal accomplishment, and the result, in part, of cross-border cooperation. (It left a different impression, however: one of near failure. It also established a sense of Canada in U.S. media as being an unreliable partner in the fight against terrorism.) Intensified cooperation followed, but there were no moves towards such change in border management as would upset the balance between the dual imperatives of economic and human security. Both governments (rightly) stressed the success of cross-border cooperation. Most proposals for radical moves to "tighten" the border (such as the initiative to introduce mandatory documentation of all entry and departures by foreigners to the United States) were dropped or diluted as unworkable or unnecessary.

This hiatus ended on September 11 when it became clear that a war, launched by invisible enemies, was to be waged on many fronts, including in North America. National security entered the mix of objectives to be pursued at the border with a vengeance.

Changes on the Border since September 11

Government actions that followed the first frenetic days have been measured and constructive. Cooperation among agencies, already closer since December 1999, was intensified and, by all accounts, works well. The U.S. Administration sent signals of determination by expanding security spending and powers as well as measures like the temporary deployment of the National Guard to provide back up at border crossings. The Canadian government took unprecedented steps to limit abuse of its refugee and immigration systems. It strengthened anti-terrorism legislation in ways that would have been politically unacceptable before September 11. It bolstered investment in security dramatically, including (but not only) at the border, in part to ensure that Canada's determination to prevent terrorists from ever reaching the U.S. border was beyond reproach.[5] Despite these improvements, fundamental change in mandate is still required. The border is still a dividing line between two compatible societies. It is still a hazard to the flows between two interdependent economies; it is still landlocked, irremediably permeable by dint of geography, and still anachronistic as a principal line defense against global threats. Many improvements are possible and in the works, both relating to improved infrastructure and better use of technology.

All these improvements will only yield optimal benefits if they are made on a shared basis rather than separately. Canadian and U.S. agencies operate, as they must, independently. They serve separate jurisdictions, are charged with protecting different space on either side of a legal line. Since our national interests in security are very similar, they inevitably spend resources in duplicating each other's efforts. They are constrained to cooperate across the line only with the greatest caution, and hence, inadequately. We will need to move beyond the conception of the border as fundamentally separating our jurisdictions, when in truth our interests largely argue for treating it as more of a shared asset.

But even with dramatic improvements in effectiveness and efficiency, the inner border, by itself, can do no more than provide modest protection for our security. The best way to ensure that it provides value, paradoxically, is to downgrade it. It should become one element in a broader arsenal to ensure continental security.

BUILD AN AREA OF MUTUAL CONFIDENCE WITHIN WHICH WE COOPERATE TO PROTECT OUR SECURITY AND WHERE BENIGN FLOWS MOVE UNIMPEDED

The leaders of our two countries (and Mexico when it is ready) should commit now, as Roosevelt and Mackenzie King committed in Ogdensburg to a new **security partnership**. Our enemy then was the Axis; ours now include global terrorism. We were engaged then in a war of great powers intent on territorial conquest; we are in a war now against shadowy enemies who rely on access to our territory for profit or victory. To respond, we should advance our existing cooperation to the development of an "Area of Mutual Confidence." Under such an umbrella, each country would act within its own territory to defend not only itself, but by extension, also its neighbor. The sovereign actions of one partner would be recognized and reciprocated by the other. Authorities of both would cooperate intensively in our shared space and offshore.

Such a partnership would not imply eliminating our "inner" border, but would allow it to perform functions that it can reasonably be expected to fulfill in a way that respects the basic balance among economic, human, and state security imperatives. It could still continue to protect such areas of difference in our policies and in our constitutional space that we each consider important to our sovereignty.

Agreement on such an approach between two (and potentially, three) partners of greatly disproportionate size and power will be, to say the least, a challenge. It would only be possible if it were conceived in a spirit of respect for and in support of our sovereignties. Its purposes would have to be clear and receive the support of our societies. It would have to be based on the partners' acceptance of agreed obligations. It would, nonetheless, be a historic achievement, inconceivable (though already necessary) before September 11. It is perhaps possible, today. What would be needed to make an "area of mutual confidence" reality?

THE FOUR RINGS OF NORTH AMERICAN SECURITY

The way to security in a globalized environment lies in building multiple borders that address the multiplicity of challenges it poses.

One way to see these multiple borders is to view them as concentric rings of action.[7]

The Rings

I.Both of our countries provide security within their territory and at external borders. This effort is already being intensified. This "domestic" action already provides the first guarantee of our societies' security. It could be made a component of a broader strategy, if the two countries formally recognized each other's efforts and built on them cooperatively.

Such an **inner ring of security**, within our sovereignties, could operate in a spirit consistent with national values and constitutional imperatives. It would do so at a level of intensity that met an agreed set of objectives. There is, in this sense, no contradiction between harmonizing our goals and mutually recognizing the validity of each other's efforts.

II.The second ring should be our **borders, reformed**. The earlier section of this paper sketched the challenges of governance on the inner border. The paper has also pointed to the need for a more complex and strategic approach to borders, inside and outside North America and in virtual space. We now have no institution to lead in formulating such a joint strategy. We must invent one. The importance of the undertaking demands it; the urgency of the moment may, uniquely, permit it.

One approach would be to assign leadership to a senior-level, Summit-mandated, bi-national body, a "Joint Border Commission." A JBC could help overcome the disconnects between national agencies, build protocols for cooperation among agencies, and stimulate the investment in technology and infrastructure at the inner border and points of entry into North America. It could also provide leadership for multilateral cooperation.

The idea of joint effort, including on the borders, is not unprecedented. Ogdensburg provided for it. The International Joint Commission, though an institution with a limited remit, provides lessons. Great shared security projects of the post war period (NORAD and the DEW Line) were built and managed jointly. The FTA/NAFTA gave our economies a joint impulse. Such a joint approach would also be consistent with modern norms of community construction, most particularly echoing the approach of the European Union, where both internal and external borders are now largely shared under the Schengen system.

The asymmetries in size and political structures will pose real challenges for such an institution working on a truly shared basis. The difficulties inherent in the challenge should not, however, deter governments from making the effort, because it would bring real benefits to both countries. The JBC, with Summit-level accountability, would allow management of the borders to be driven by the long term. It would allow the communities most directly affected by the border a means to participate in its management. Lastly, it would be a powerful symbol, expressing the mature partnership between two uniquely kindred societies. These new North American borders, given a common impulse, should be the second ring assuring our security.

   III. The third would lie offshore. The notion that a line around the continent would, of itself, defend North America, is fanciful. This is a world where threats come from networks without geography. Offshore cooperation then would need to take the form of networks to monitor and anticipate threatening flows.

There is already considerable, if greatly uneven, information sharing among authorities worldwide. Canada and the United States should initiate an institutionalized, extended, and intensified approach to networking. The effort needs the involvement of all societies concerned about global threats from terrorism and the traffic in drugs, people, hazardous waste, and illegal and corrupting capital. That means pretty much the whole world, and cooperation on that scale could best be built on multilateral principles and structures. Our partnership with Mexico (through the Puebla process) and with Europe would appear to be among the first upon which to build toward this goal.

This **international security cooperation** would then be the third ring of our security.

   IV. There is a fourth ring: increasing "human security" outside our area.

Terrorism is a monstrous perversion in the conduct of human affairs. It is perpetrated by individuals who have to hide in, and draw sustenance from, a broader environment of resentment created by want, insecurity, ignorance, and intolerance. There is, more broadly, ample misery distributed through the world to foment threats other than terrorism to our security: drug cultivation provides what is often the only alternative to absolute poverty. The illegal migrations that so concern our societies are the tip of an iceberg. Over 150 million people are on the move involuntarily around the world. No amount of border restrictions will stem such a tide, caused as it is by material misery, lack of basic rights, and paralyzing personal insecurity.[8] The disregard of human, civil, and property rights; corruption in the practice of democracy; ineffective legal and public security systems; pandemics that decimate populations; environmental degradation; and lack of economic and educational opportunity are all real threats, direct and indirect, to our security in a globalized world.

Given this reality, the last ring of security has to be **a renewed commitment to action for positive change in the broader world**. This is not a new imperative. What it needs is not to be forgotten as we focus in on the threats we see as imminent. It needs more than that; it needs our leadership, commitment, resources, and institutions to implement it.

CREATE A PUBLIC DISCOURSE TO BUILD CONSENSUS IN FAVOR OF A NEW APPROACH TO NORTH AMERICAN SECURITY

Decisions of the kind advanced here will (to understate the point) be politically challenging. A structured ventilation of the issues as well as the opportunity for all affected communities and interests to make their inputs will be important to ensuring that decisions reflect a politically acceptable, and hence sustainable, consensus. The CUSP forum made a start in stimulating a more limited discourse. Governments will need to consider what level of engagement they will wish to stimulate with parliaments, sub-national jurisdictions stakeholders, and publics.

CONCLUSION

The idea of "borders" we now have is obsolete. Our shared border in particular, is a weak instrument for the protection of our societies. The best way to address the real threats that we share is to address them on their own terms, through a mix of domestic action, continental partnership, and global cooperation. For the short term, in order to ensure that our shared border is efficient enough not to affect our economic security adversely and acts as a meaningful filter for threats against our societies, we must invest in and reform it. For the longer term, we must reinvent our borders, both those that lie between us and those that we present to the world, and make them part of a broader framework of security and cooperation in the world. That broader framework will require a vigorous commitment to multilateral cooperation to address both direct and the less direct threats to our security.

The issues raised here are public policy challenges whose successful management would need sustained commitment. Our political leaders need to consider how to engage with stakeholders and publics to secure it.

ENDNOTES

1 "Building a Border for the 21st Century," CUSP Forum Report, December 2000. http:/www.dfait-maeci.gc.ca/geo/usa/Canadian-e.asp.

2 The land border also had another human security function before the Civil War; it provided a fence beyond which escaped slaves found refuge.

3 Repeated efforts were made later in that century and well into the next to revive reciprocity, but the border remained a formidable barrier to commerce until the FTA/NAFTA eroded this function, at least theoretically, to near irrelevance.

4 Though we have shared in air defense through NORAD and more generally, through NATO.

5 It is possible that such decisive action has overcome, or at least balanced, the negative brand the U.S. media have assigned to Canada in this area and has allowed security cooperation to proceed on a basis of mutual confidence, but this cannot be taken for granted.

6 With apologies to Tolkien.

7 The military dimension of continental security is a subject too important and complex to touch on within the limits of this paper. It is self-evident that military cooperation is already, and should continue to be, a critical component of efforts to protect the security of the continent.

8 Our societies provide an indispensable haven. They also rely on immigration to sustain them.

A PRIMER ON
AIRPORT SECURITY

Darryl Jenkins

The purpose of this paper is to discuss changes that have been mandated at airports because of the events of September 11, 2001. These changes will be compared to best practices used by Israel, Germany, and other European countries. This paper will proceed in the following manner: first, I will discuss the changes mandated by the Transportation Security Act of 2001 and signed into law by President Bush on November 11, 2001. I will then describe the airports' current security system and how it will change in the next couple of years. Finally, I will conclude with a discussion of best practices and compare them to those mandated by the law.

It is concluded that while the recent changes will have marginal benefits to the security system, it is still based on a flawed foundation: that of baggage screening rather than person screening. The biggest problem with baggage screening is that it is boring and repetitive, and therefore prone to error. As the law mandates better-educated screeners, we may actually see worse security, as the work is too mundane to hold their attention.

Another significant problem with the security procedures is that they do not take into account how terrorism has changed in the last decade. The most significant improvements in security may have come through pilots becoming non-passive and passengers becoming aggressive towards terrorism. The necessary element for airport security – that of intelligence gathering at the federal level – has not yet been addressed.

THE AVIATION AND TRANSPORTATION SECURITY ACT

On November 19, 2001, President George W. Bush signed the Aviation and Transportation Security Act (the Act, Pub.L. 107-71) into law. This comprehensive statute established the Transportation Security Administration (TSA), as well as the position of under secretary of transportation for security, and required the federal government to over-haul its approach to securing all modes of transportation.

The TSA will assume responsibility for security beginning this year. The bulk of the new agency's authority is centered on the air transportation system, particularly protecting against terrorist threats, sabotage, and other acts of violence. A core element of this aviation security regime is the screening of passengers and property at all airports that provide commercial air service.

To execute this complex function, TSA will hire and deploy security screeners and supervisors at 429 airports over the next 10 months. Based on the dual requirements of protecting the system and moving passengers who present no threat through security checkpoints efficiently, the screener workforce is likely to exceed 30,000 people. In addition, TSA will employ thousands of Federal Law Enforcement Officers (LEOs), as well as intelligence and support personnel.

Given its size, the number of passengers with whom it will come in direct contact, and the importance of its role in ongoing operations, the screener workforce represents the core of the agency. To ensure the protection and smooth operation of the aviation system, and the long-term success of TSA, screeners must receive premium-quality, intense, and measurable training on the range of responsibilities and scenarios they are likely to face. At the time of the writing of this article, the following items under the law have been carried out, and the following remain to be completed.

IN PLACE

- Increased use of a computer program that identifies potentially suspicious travelers for bag searches or interviews

- As of January 18, 2002, all checked luggage must be screened by either explosive detection machines, matching the bag to the passenger, hand searches, or the use of bomb-sniffing dogs.

- Increased use of random searches of carry-on bags

- Limits on carry-on items

- Government-issued ID necessary for boarding

- Parking and curbside access will be limited.

- Armed National Guardsmen stationed at security checkpoints

- Stricter procedures at checkpoints, including frequent hand-wand checks and pat-downs at many large airports

- FAA agents will shut down concourses and hold flights if they observe flaws in security procedures.

- Cockpit doors remain shut; flight crews inflexible about in-flight rules

- Increased presence of Federal Armed Marshals on some flights

- The FAA requires criminal background checks of all employees with access to secure areas at airports.

- Bags and passengers screened at small airports are not required to be rechecked before boarding connecting flights.

REMAINS UNDONE

- No additional training has been provided for checkpoint screeners.

- Checkpoint screeners still have no health benefits.

CURRENT SECURITY PRACTICES IN DOMESTIC AIRPORTS

Millions of people fly every day. The vast majority of them are law-abiding folks who have no intention of harming anyone. But there is always the possibility that a terrorist or a criminal is hidden among the masses. Also, many people with no intent to cause harm may accidentally carry hazardous material onto the plane. To avoid these problems, airport security is an important part of any airport. The fact that the plurality of people who pass through checkpoints will bring no danger to the system brings us to the most important problem in maintaining security: human factors. The likelihood of any one screener ever catching a terrorist is remote in the extreme. So while terrorism causes the push for increased security, screeners will have to deal with more routine daily operational problems. Knowing this, they will lack the necessary tension to fully conduct their duties. To overcome this, audits, etc., are conducted. The problem with the previous system was high turnover; screeners never had any motivation to do their jobs well, as the job was only a stepping stone to another low-paying job. However, tension is necessary to perform these types of tasks well. It is assumed that this will always be a problem, but hopefully, it will be less of a problem in the new regime.

Since this paper is concerned mostly with terrorism, I will ignore the other security aspects like air rage, disgruntled employees, etc., and concentrate solely on preventing terrorist acts and the current and proposed procedures to do this.

If we try to imagine a terrorist attempting to blow up or hijack a plane, we need to consider all of the different techniques the terrorist might use to get a bomb into position, and whether the new procedures could stop him or her. A terrorist could:

- Plant a bomb in an unsuspecting passenger's luggage

- Smuggle a bomb in his luggage

- Strap a bomb or gun onto his body

- Walk onto the tarmac by hopping a fence and approach a plane from the ground

- Like the terrorists on September 11, 2001, work through the system as it exists and know all of its weak points

The first line of security at an airport is confirming identity. For domestic flights, this is done by checking a photo ID, such as a driver's license. When people travel internationally, they need to present a passport. Confirming a person's identity is difficult; it could be one of the greatest tasks in the new security regime. Even fingerprints cannot confirm a person's identity, but they can reveal whether or not a person was in jail. The identity portion of security is important, as it gives us leads about certain people's backgrounds. Because identity is uncertain, profiling takes on increased importance.

During the check-in process, the attendant asks security questions:

- Has your luggage been in your possession at all times?

- Has anyone given you anything or asked you to carry on or check any items for them?

While we often ridicule these questions when going through check-in, they are very important, as a tactic terrorists occasionally use is to hide a bomb inside an unsuspecting person's luggage. Another tactic is to give something, perhaps a toy or stuffed animal, to someone who is about to board a plane. That object, although it seems innocent, may actually be a bomb or other harmful device.

The Civil Aviation Security (CAS), a division of the Federal Aviation Administration, establishes guidelines and requirements for airport security. CAS has three main objectives for airport security:

- To prevent attacks on airports or aircraft

- To prevent accidents and fatalities due to transport of hazardous materials

- To ensure safety and security of passengers

FAA agents working under CAS are located at every major airport for immediate response to possible threats. Most major airports also have an entire police force monitoring all facets of the facility, and require background checks on all airport personnel, from baggage handlers to security-team members, before they can be employed. All airport personnel have photo-ID cards with their name, position, and access privileges clearly labeled. One of the biggest problems with the new security workforce is the time required to do background checks – as the law has mandated 10-year instead of five-year background checks, they will take as long as 10 months per individual.

A fence generally secures the entire perimeter of an airport. It restricts access to the runways, cargo-handling facilities, and terminal gates. However, fences are easily breached and are seldom patrolled. The purpose of the perimeter is to channel all public access through the terminal, where every person must walk through a metal detector and all carry-on items must go through an X-ray machine. Currently, checked baggage is screened only on a random basis, with the law mandating 100 percent screening within one year. This will be difficult, as the companies that are now certificated to build these machines do not have the production capability to do this.

Almost all airport metal detectors are based on pulse induction (PI). Typical PI systems use a coil of wire on one side of the arch as the transmitter and receiver. This technology sends powerful, short bursts (pulses) of current through the coil of wire. Each pulse generates a brief magnetic field. When the pulse ends, the magnetic field reverses polarity and collapses very suddenly, resulting in a sharp electrical spike. This spike lasts a few microseconds (millionths of a second) and causes another current to run through the coil. This subsequent current is called the reflected pulse and lasts only about 30 microseconds. Another pulse is then sent and the process repeats. A typical PI-based metal detector sends about 100 pulses per second, but the number can vary greatly based on the manufacturer and model, ranging from about 25 pulses per second to over 1,000.

If a metal object passes through the metal detector, the pulse creates an opposite magnetic field in the object. When the pulse's magnetic field collapses, causing the reflected pulse, the magnetic field of the object makes it take longer for the reflected pulse to completely disappear. This process works something like echoes: if you yell in a room with only a few hard surfaces, you probably hear only a very brief echo, or you may not hear one at all. But if you yell into a room with a lot of hard surfaces, the echo lasts longer. In a PI metal detector, the magnetic fields from target objects add their "echo" to the reflected pulse, making it last a fraction longer than it would without them.

A sampling circuit in the metal detector is set to monitor the length of the reflected pulse. By comparing it to the expected length, the circuit can determine if another magnetic field has caused the reflected pulse to take longer to decay. If the decay of the reflected pulse takes more than a few microseconds longer than normal, there is probably a metal object interfering with it.

The sampling circuit sends the tiny, weak signals that it monitors to a device call an integrator. The integrator reads the signals from the sampling circuit, amplifying and converting them to direct current (DC). The DC's voltage is connected to an audio circuit, where it is changed into a tone that the metal detector uses to indicate that a target object has been found. If an item is found, passengers are asked to remove any metal objects from their person and step through again. If the metal detector continues to indicate the presence of metal, the attendant uses a handheld detector, based on the same PI technology, to isolate the cause.

Many of the newer metal detectors on the market are multi-zone. This means that they have multiple transmit and receive coils, each one at a different height. Basically, it is like having several metal detectors in a single unit.

While a person steps through the metal detector, his carry-on items are going through the X-ray system. A conveyor belt carries each item past an X-ray machine. X-rays are like light in that they are electromagnetic waves, but they are more energetic, so they can penetrate many materials. The machines used in airports are usually based on a dual-energy X-ray system. This system has a single X-ray source sending out X-rays typically in the range of 140 to 160 kilovolt peak (KVP). KVP refers to the amount of penetration an X-ray makes. The higher the KVP, the further the X-ray penetrates.

After the X-rays pass through the item, they are picked up by a detector. This detector then passes the X-rays on to a filter, which blocks out the lower-energy X-rays. The remaining high-energy X-rays hit a second detector. A computer circuit compares the pick-ups of the two detectors to better represent low-energy objects, such as most organic materials.

Since different materials absorb X-rays at different levels, the image on the monitor lets the machine operator see distinct items inside bags. Items are typically colored on the display monitor, based on the range of energy that passes through the object, to represent one of three main categories:

- Organic

- Inorganic

- Metal

While the colors used to signify "inorganic" and "metal" may vary between manufacturers, all X-ray systems use shades of orange to represent "organic." This is because most explosives are organic. Machine operators are trained to look for suspicious items – and not just obviously suspicious items like guns or knives, but also anything that could be a component of an improvised explosive device (IED). Since there is no such thing as a commercially available bomb, most terrorists and hijackers use IEDs to gain control. An IED can be made in an astounding variety of ways, from basic pipe bombs to sophisticated, electronically controlled component bombs.

A common misconception is that the X-ray machine used to check carry-on items damages film and electronic media. In actuality, all modern carry-on X-ray systems are considered film-safe. This means that the amount of X-ray radiation is not high enough to damage photographic film. Since electronic media can withstand much more radiation than film can, it is also safe from damage. However, the CT scanner and many of the high-energy X-ray systems used to examine checked baggage can damage film (electronic media is still safe), so it should be carried on the plane.

Electronic items, such as laptop computers, have so many different items packed into a relatively small area that it can be difficult to determine if a bomb is hidden within the device. That is why screeners sometimes ask passengers to turn on their laptops. But even this is not sufficient evidence, since a skilled criminal could hide a bomb within a working electronic device. For that reason, many airports also have a chemical sniffer. This is essentially an automated chemistry lab in a box. At random intervals, or if there is reason to suspect an electronic device someone is carrying, the security attendant quickly swipes a cloth over the device and places the cloth on the sniffer. The sniffer analyzes the cloth for any trace residue of the types of chemicals used to make bombs. If there is any residue, the sniffer warns the security attendant of a potential bomb.

In addition to passenger baggage, most planes carry enormous amounts of cargo. All of this cargo has to be checked before it is loaded.

Most airports use one of three systems to do this:

- Medium X-ray systems – These are fixed systems that can scan an entire pallet of cargo for suspicious items.

- Mobile X-ray systems – A large truck carries a complete X-ray scanning system. The truck drives very slowly beside a parked truck to scan the entire contents of that truck for suspicious items.

- Fixed-site systems – This is an entire building that is basically one huge X-ray scanner. A tractor-trailer is pulled into the building and the entire truck is scanned at one time.

One old-fashioned method of bomb detection still works as well or better than most high-tech systems – the use of trained dogs. These special dogs, called K-9 units, have been trained to sniff out the specific odors emitted by chemicals that are used to make bombs, as well the odors of other items such as drugs. Incredibly fast and accurate, a K-9 barks at a suspicious bag or package, alerting the human companion that this item needs to be investigated. One of the problems we have discovered with using dogs is that they find this work as boring as humans do and are generally only good for one hour a day.

In addition to an X-ray system, many airports also use larger scanners. The first security inspection checked bags pass through depends on the airport. In the United States, most major airports have a computer tomography (CT) scanner. A CT scanner is a hollow tube that surrounds the bag. An X-ray mechanism revolves slowly around it, bombarding it with X-rays and recording the resulting data. The CT scanner uses all of this data to create a very detailed tomogram (slice) of the bag. The scanner is able to calculate the mass and density of individual objects in the bag based on this tomogram. If an object's mass/density falls within the range of a dangerous material, the CT scanner warns the operator of a potential hazardous object.

CT scanners are slow compared to other types of baggage-scanning systems, so they are not used to check every bag. Instead, only bags that the computer flags as "suspicious" are checked. These flags are triggered by any anomaly that shows up in the reservation or check-in process. For example, if a person buys a one-way ticket and pays cash, this is considered atypical and could cause the computer to flag that person. When this happens, that person's checked bags are immediately sent through the CT scanner, which is usually located somewhere near the ticketing counter.

In most other countries, particularly in Europe, all baggage is run through a scanning system. These systems are basically larger versions of the X-ray system used for carry-on items. The main differences are that they are high-speed, automated machines integrated into the normal baggage-handling system and the KVP range of the X-rays is higher.

While most of the things that cannot be taken on board an airplane are fairly obvious (guns, knives, explosives), there are others that most people would not think of – who would have thought a smoke detector could be considered hazardous? A person could be fined up to $27,500 for transporting a hazardous material on a passenger plane without declaring it. In a plane, a can of shaving cream is more dangerous than a bomb without a detonator attached. If a plane has structural problems and goes into decompression, any aerosol can inside it would explode.

As another safety precaution, aviation workers, from flight attendants to security personnel, are trained to react to certain words, such as "bomb," "hijack" or "gun." A person could be immediately removed from the plane and quite possibly arrested for saying these words, even in jest.

FAA AIR TRAVELER ADVISORY OF OCTOBER 8, 2001

On October 8, 2001, the FAA issued the following tips to help air travelers meet and assist the heightened security measures implemented since the September 11 attacks:

Carry-On Baggage

- Air travelers are limited to one carry-on bag and one personal item (such as a purse or briefcase) on all flights.

Allow Extra Time

- Heightened security measures require more time to properly screen travelers. Travelers should contact their airline to find out how early they should arrive at the airport.

- Take public transportation to the airport if possible. Parking and curbside access is likely to be controlled and limited.

- Curbside check-in is available on an airline-by-airline basis. Travelers should contact their airline to see if it is in place at their airport.

Check-in

- A government-issued ID (federal, state, or local) is required. Travelers may be asked to show this ID at subsequent points, such as at the gate, along with their boarding passes.

- Automated check-in kiosks are available for airlines that have appropriate security measures in place. Travelers interested in this option should check with their airline.

- E-ticket travelers should check with their airline to make sure they have proper documentation. Written confirmation, such as a letter from the airline acknowledging the reservation, may be required.

Screener Checkpoints

- Only ticketed passengers are allowed beyond the screener checkpoints, except for those with specific medical or parental needs.

- All electronic items, such as laptops and cell phones, may be subjected to additional screening. Passengers should be prepared to remove laptops from their travel cases so that both can be X-rayed separately.

- Passengers should limit the amount of jewelry or other metal objects they wear.

- Travelers should remove all metal objects prior to passing through the metal detectors in order to facilitate the screening process.

AIRPORT SECURITY IN OTHER COUNTRIES: BEST PRACTICES

This section will compare some of the security procedures in Europe and Israel. The public literature for this section is taken from General Accounting Office reports (GAO), and most of the information comes from *Aviation Security: Long-Standing Problems Impair Airport Screeners' Performance RCED-00-75 June 28, 2000*. Little else is available on this subject, but the following information can be used to compare other countries to the United States:

1. The two most important reasons for screeners' poor performance are the rapid turnover among them and human factor problems. Turnover exceeds 100 percent per year at most airports, leaving few screeners with much experience at the largest hubs.

2. The main reasons for the high turnover rate are low wages and the human factor issues – those of repetitive, boring, stressful work requiring constant vigilance.

3. Belgium, Canada, France, the Netherlands, and the United Kingdom conduct their screening differently, performing regular "pat downs" of passengers.

4. These countries also pay their screeners more and provide benefits.

5. All of these countries have better screener performance (they are twice as good as Americans in detecting hazardous material), but still have a large number of dangerous materials going through their checkpoints.

6. In addition, the five European countries only allow ticketed passengers beyond checkpoints. This practice was started in the United States only after 9-11.

7. The European countries also require five times more training than their American counterparts, which is still by many measures insignificant, as it only requires a couple of weeks to begin work.

8. The Israeli system is one of passenger screening rather than baggage screening.

There is also the problem of governance. Under the new legislation, the United States is moving away from airport-controlled security towards government-controlled security. Yet we know few details about how the United States will run its new operations, as little information is available at this time, and outside contractors will be required for many years to make the transition. By comparison, these countries use the following governance:

Throughout all of the **United Kingdom**, the primary responsibility for airport security measures falls to the airport authority – the entity that operates the airport. The airport authority – not the airlines – hires private security contractors to staff security checkpoints. In addition, there is a significant police presence in the screening areas to support the private security workforce.

Three government ministries control security at all airports in **Amsterdam**. Working together, these ministries hire private contractors to provide airport security services. The contractors work in unison with a local police force to handle all airport security checkpoints.

As in the UK, the airport authorities in **Ireland** have the responsibility of providing security at all the country's airports. The security workers are direct employees of the airport authority. This security force works together with the airport police force and private security contractors at all security checkpoints.

The Ministry of the Interior in **Germany** has the charge of providing airport security nationwide. The Interior Ministry hires private contractors to provide security services at the major German airports. The private security contractors are supervised at the checkpoints by a local police force.

Some of the highest levels of airport security are provided in **Israel**. Like in Europe, the airport authority is responsible for security measures. The Israel Airports Authority also has help from the country's internal security service. In addition, these two entities have extra security support from private security contractors hired by El Al Airlines.

DISCUSSION

There is little, if anything, about the way the United States domestic airline industry has conducted airport security that is worthy of emulation. At the same time, most of the changes that are being implemented under the new legislation would not have deterred the hijackers on September 11, 2001. There are a number of problems that the new legislation does not address:

1. The changing face of terrorism

2. The human factor problems

3. Who is going to pay for all of this?

4. The role of the federal government in gathering intelligence

The terrorists who acted on September 11 were different from those the United States had ever seen before. They were well paid and had strategies that worked. They spent years in training, and the U.S. government had no indications of their plan. Their ability to formulate these plans and keep them secret for so long shows a governance capacity among terrorists that is quite impressive. Also, there was not a rush to admit guilt as there has been in the past. During the early 1990s, terrorists around the world readily admitted to their actions after the attacks had taken place. This has signaled a changeover in terrorists' strategies, the difference being that religiously motivated terrorists gain approval from divinity, which always knows what is going on, so they do not need CNN to announce their triumphs to the world. This makes terrorists deadlier enemies for the future.

The failure to detect terrorist plans stems from direct policies implemented by the Congress to cut security and intelligence gathering, most likely because the country became complacent to threats during the late 1990s. The economy was booming, lower taxes became the mantra, and national security became a very low priority. However, the real reason that the events of 9-11 did not happen earlier is simply that we have been lucky. The luck of the draw does not imply security on our part.

Another problem in the new security world is that of human factors. It is important to recognize in any airport security discussion that gazing into a computer screen at three-dimensional objects presented in two dimensions is problematic. The first problem is the absolute boredom of the task, and the second problem is one of interpretation.

The first part of the problem is best handled by using screeners who are mentally challenged, as they are better able to attend to repetitive tasks. At the same time, this makes it easier for the majority of travelers with no regard for the system, terrorists, and others to circumvent the system. Yet more intelligent screeners, most likely, do not perform the job as well due to the monotony. We need to find ways to motivate screeners and rotate them through a variety of tasks in order to keep them fresh. The human factor problems show how wise the Israelis are. Their system is based on screening people, rather than baggage. This does not mean they do not screen baggage; they do, but they spend most of their resources doing interviews. While it is unlikely that the United States will or can adopt the Israeli system, it can implement a derivative. Interviews seem to deter terrorists the most – the fear of being caught, by a human, in a situation wherein they have no resources for escape.

At the same time, the more intelligent screener is better capable of doing pat downs and conducting intelligence gathering (interviewing passengers) to access threats. The predicament is an interesting one, as the qualifications for the best security personnel (intelligence, conversation, etc.) are the opposite of those required by a system grounded in checking baggage.

The third problem – that of paying for all the needed changes to secure airports – is daunting. Discussing the changes made at Heathrow airport in London some years ago can put this into perspective. Heathrow's changes cost over $300 million. Adding to this the new security equipment needed at 420 airports results in a staggering amount of money. Senators, who agreed 100-0 on the new measures, will fall apart during the next year figuring out how to pay for their laws.

The last issue – that of integrating the new airport security people with federal intelligence gathering – is also daunting, as the history of agency conflicts and turf is one of stove piping, and little cooperation could be one of the biggest problems to overcome.

Meanwhile, things have changed since 9-11 that may be more important than anything the federal government has done or can do. These are:

1. The aggressive attitudes of commercial airline pilots

2. The aggressive attitudes of passengers and flight attendants

Pilots' attitudes are important, as in the past they were taught to be passive during hijackings. The reasoning was that if they cooperated with the hijacker, there was greater likelihood they and their passengers would escape without any harm. The events of 9-11 changed this. Pilots, when alerted to hijackings, can put a plane in extremely unnatural attitudes that make it impossible for anybody to move the plane around. We have also seen a marked change in flight attendants' and passengers' attitudes. This was seen in the case of the American Airlines flight from Paris, when the flight attendant acted heroically and the passengers came to her aid.

We will never know for sure what happened to the United Airlines plane that crashed in Pennsylvania, but the passengers' actions – whatever they were – changed passengers' actions in hijacking situations forever.

KNOWLEDGE RELATED TO A PURPOSE: DATA-MINING TO DETECT TERRORISM

Stan Hawthorne

September 11 created uncertainty in America – uncertainly about the government's ability to protect its citizens from those who would do them harm. Accordingly, the American public is questioning as never before the government's ability to counter these terrorists' acts. Additionally, they express frustration with the government's continued warnings that the terrorists may strike again without being given any specifics. Exacerbating this is the fact that countering acts such as 9-11 is an intelligence game, and one that by its very definition is not, and cannot, be transparent to the public at large. They have a right to question, and the answer lies in the government's ability to reestablish the feeling of security and self-confidence held by the American public on September 10.

Countering terrorism first requires detection – detection of either the person's intent to execute a terrorist act or the means by which that person intends to deliver the terrorist act – i.e. a bomb, a biological weapon, a hijacked airplane. The foundation of detection is intelligence. There is mounting frustration that while spending billions on intelligence, we can still fail. The business of intelligence is not simply data or information; it is a process where *data* is transformed into *knowledge related to a purpose* (stop terrorists, prevent fraud, change leadership, etc.). If data is not transformed into substantive information and is not accessible to those charged with the mission, appropriate action cannot be taken.

To do a better job of detection, the government must consolidate and manage all available data[1] of various forms – imagery, human intelligence, communication, intelligence summaries, for example – in a way that makes all known information about an individual or group who proposes to do harm available for decision-making. This consolidation can be accomplished using modern technology in a data-mining/data-warehousing environment. In this paper, we present such a consolidation as an evolutionary process wherein rapid deployment will provide useable information to combat terrorism in a short time period. Thereafter, it can be refined and evolved to a more comprehensive knowledge management system.

To illustrate where and why the government's current methods of assembling and disseminating intelligence falls short, and how these challenges can better be met, we will take as an example the role of intelligence data management in border control. Border control is, of course, just one of several strategic and tactical challenges where better intelligence data management is needed.

FRAGMENTED INTELLIGENCE

The events of September 11 indicate that while the United States may have had the necessary intelligence in aggregate, current fragmentation of that intelligence across government entities does not provide anyone with the total perspective. News reports continue to gain momentum that the "government" was informed on numerous occasions that a terrorist attack was imminent. Yet is seems that whatever data or intelligence may have been known was not analyzed into a single unified picture. The dispersal of this data among numerous individuals and agencies or departments is an inherent result of the stove-piped nature of our national security and law enforcement intelligence infrastructure.

Two notorious U.S. failures in the area of border security further highlight this problem: the well-reported cases of Rafael Resendez, a serial killer, and of two Palestinians who attempted to bomb the New York City subway system in 1997.

The Border Patrol apprehended Resendez on seven separate occasions in 1998 and each time he was allowed to return to Mexico. The Border Patrol agents did not know that Resendez had a long criminal history in the United States (eight convictions in seven different states) and had been previously deported three times. In January 1999, he was identified as a suspect in a murder in Texas. That investigation eventually led to his being identified as a serial killer and placed on the FBI's Ten Most Wanted list in May 1999. Even with this high criminal profile and notoriety, when the Border Patrol apprehended Resendez again the following month, they once again allowed him to return to Mexico.

A second failure was uncovered during an investigation by the Department of Justice Inspector General of how individuals arrested for attempting to bomb the New York City subway system gained entry to the United States. (The IG's office issued a report on its investigation in March 1998.) In the course of the investigation, the IG learned that one of the individuals had sought asylum in Canada on the basis of being persecuted by the Israeli government as a suspected member of the Palestinian Hamas terrorist group. Prior to being arrested for the attempted bombing, he had twice been returned by the Border Patrol to Canada even though he had already been convicted in Canada for other offenses. On his third attempt to enter the U.S. illegally, he was detained and released on bond awaiting a deportation hearing. It was only because he failed to appear on the bond hearing that he, together with another individual who was also in this country illegally, was arrested in the bombing plot.

These are but two publicized examples of the failure of the existing structure to control our borders. Prior to September 11, the cost of this failure was probably a few hundred lives lost per year and multiple thousands of crimes committed by aliens in this country.[2] Since that terrible day, the cost of this failure has simply become too great both in terms of lives lost and the probability that there will be future attacks if the problem is not solved.

CAUSES ROOTED IN DEMOCRACY

There are many root causes for the apparent intelligence failure leading to September 11, many of which are founded in the very fundamentals of the democracy we hold so dear. We are an open society that demands that our government operate in full view of the American voter, and, while this is a basic tenet in our society that cannot be denigrated, it also presents obstacles when combating factions who don't play by the same rulebook.

Lack of a National Police Force: Historically, the United States has placed a high emphasis on not having a national police force in either reality or perception. Although this is regarded as a hallmark of a free society, it means that our system for investigating and preventing criminal acts is spread among many departments and agencies at both the national and state levels. Additionally, the intelligence community is spread across both civilian and defense departments and agencies, creating a wealth of inefficiencies and conflicts. Changes in jurisdiction as an individual moves from place to place further contribute to the lack of a consistent, efficient process for handling, integrating, and analyzing the basic foundation of detection – intelligence.

Law-Enforcement Requirements: Currently within the federal government alone there are roughly 40 separate entities engaged in intelligence gathering. These entities at times work at cross-purposes insofar as the target of one investigation may be a confidential informant providing useful information to another agency. Undeniably, the activities of these groups at times place both the confidential informant and the federal agents in physical danger, leading to a hesitancy to fully share and disclose information among the competing parties. However, oftentimes one or more entities may have information about an individual serving as a confidential informant to a different agency, which, if known, may prove useful to that agency. Obviously, it would behoove all parties to be fully informed. But process and technological challenges make that difficult.

Classification and Compartmentalization of Data: Much of the intelligence information that is critical is the product of processing highly classified data. Raw data and subsequent analyses are classified for various reasons, including protecting a source or technology advantage. Classified information is often "compartmented" allowing access to a minimum number of people deemed to have a "need to know." Because of the potentially disastrous consequences resulting from compromised sources or methods, agencies producing highly sensitive intelligence information are understandably reluctant to share some data. Second, the nature of the information to be shared and the collaborative processes desired mandate secure connectivity between all nodes of the network. The potential for compromise precludes hosting on the World Wide Web and necessitates the latest and most sophisticated firewalls and information security processes and system.

Judicial Process: Further complicating the issue of detection is the judicial process of a democracy such as our own. In most instances, if information is to be used in the prosecution of a suspect, the attorney representing the defendant has the right to full disclosure and authentication of the information. Yet it is often impossible to disclose intelligence information without at the same time betraying the sources and methods by which such information was developed. Making this information publicly available often destroys the usefulness of this approach in the future, and, in extreme cases, may place certain parties in jeopardy due to retaliation.

Desire for Full Disclosure: Another factor that has grown in the past years is the desire on the part of the American public to know the details of what its government is doing and have total transparency to the activities of its agents. Today's approach to journalistic reporting has contributed to this demand by the public for total transparency. Terrorist attacks of recent years and increased competition for scarce resources have compelled the Congress for more timely access to more intelligence information. Obviously in many instances, this desire for full disclosure counters the need to run covert intelligence operations. Historically, some sources and methods for obtaining useful information were simply not utilized due to the possible negative ramifications that could have resulted if such sources and methods became public knowledge. However, September 11 has created an unequalled level of solidarity among the American people and within Congress, wherein intelligence operations may be less likely to be compromised, either knowingly or unknowingly.

BORDER CONTROL: WE DON'T KNOW WHO'S HERE

Since September 11, the administration and the Congress have focused their attention on visa application and visa enforcement as a partial solution to controlling U.S. borders. Under the current statutory structure, responsibility for enforcing the laws concerning who can legally enter the United States is vested in the attorney general as a domestic law enforcement matter. The Immigration and Naturalization Service (INS) is primarily charged with this responsibility. Positively identifying individuals seeking to enter the United States and knowing who is here are not trivial tasks. In testimony before the House Judiciary Committee in February 2000, the INS estimated that there were more than 525 million applicants for entry into the United States in FY 1999.[3]

Most persons traversing our borders do so through visas whose issuance is the responsibility of the State Department, and this is where the current approach first starts to break down. The central problem is that there are numerous databases containing differing data about the same individuals, and these databases do not share data.

- **The State Department Bureau of Intelligence and Research** maintains a classified database containing records on individuals who have been identified as involved in terrorist activities. The INS has not previously had direct access to this database.

- There is also the **INS Interagency Border Inspection System,** which contains information on individuals who may be inadmissible or removable from the United States, or subject to enforcement actions by another U.S. law enforcement agency.

- A third system, the **INS IDENT system,** is an automated fingerprint identification system that the INS uses during secondary inspections[4] to match an individual's fingerprints to those of known illegal aliens. However, this database of known "illegals" is not connected to the FBI's Automated Fingerprint Identification System that is designed to contain fingerprints on all individuals convicted of a felony in the United States. (As a result of the Resendez case, the Department of Justice has undertaken a plan to link these two systems.)

It has become clear that no U.S. government agency has the capability of tracking the entry or exit of foreigners who legally (or illegally) enter the United States. We don't know who is in the United States – much less where they are. According to INS testimony before the House Immigration Subcommittee in 1999 the INS "only collects arrival and departure data on approximately 10 percent of foreign visitors."[5]

Most visitors enter from Canada and Mexico, and most are not required to have visas. Foreigners are currently tracked only if they are under scrutiny of the FBI's counter-intelligence division or arrested by local police for a criminal or traffic violation. Information on foreigners who enter the United States depends on them truthfully filling out a form called an I-94, which asks for minimal information such as an address at which the visitor is staying in the United States. No database of biometric information, such as fingerprints or face geometry exists on foreigners (i.e., non-immigrants, or individuals seeking temporary entry into the United States) entering and leaving the country.

MINING DATA FOR INTELLIGENCE

September 11 changed many aspects of this situational analysis. While we are still faced with conflicting agendas of many departments and agencies, there is a growing public demand that these entities operate in concert. Whether true or not, the newscasters' nightly disclosure that one government agency had certain data about one or more of the terrorists that, if known by another agency, may have prevented the events is difficult for the typical American to accept. Equally difficult to accept is the fact that some of these perpetrators may have been in this country illegally, and, even so, could not only go about their activities undeterred but could even participate in what the average person would deem to be "suspicious" activity.

The first step in mitigating these systemic issues was President Bush's creation of a Cabinet-level position dedicated to "Homeland Security" and the appointment of Governor Tom Ridge of Pennsylvania to lead this effort. Prior attempts to overcome the issues of working across the multiple organizations and jurisdictions have failed to achieve the desired results due to the lack of authority – an issue that can be resolved through the elevation of the responsibility and authority to a Cabinet level. However, simply creating an additional Cabinet position will have little impact without empowering the position with a commensurate transfer of the resources necessary to accomplish the mission.

Ultimately, the prevention of terrorist acts is best achieved by the absolute identification and apprehension of those persons intending to commit such acts. And, absolute identification through biometric technology[6] is achievable. But the adoption, acquisition, and the necessary cross-boundary implementation of such technology and the creation of biometric databases of those who intend to do harm cannot be done in the short term. This paper focuses on steps that can be accomplished in a relatively short timeframe, with an approach that can be refined and enhanced to meet the needs of the longer term as well.

The immediate focus should be to efficiently interact with the multiple entities possessing data which, when viewed collectively, may allow the government to identify the potential terrorist. Although this is not an undertaking without pitfalls, technology advances provide the means to efficiently achieve such an objective through automated feeds from the entities[7] into a large-scale data warehouse. The concept would be that of "mining" data from the numerous agencies, departments, state and local law enforcement entities, and foreign members of the anti-terrorism coalition. This warehouse then becomes a master set of data, giving the Office of Homeland Security a comprehensive profile of suspected terrorists and terrorist organizations. A comparable unclassified system for identifying individuals wanted by the police, stolen vehicles, missing persons, and other data of interest to law enforcement has existed in this country for years at the FBI's National Criminal Information Center (NCIC). Thousands of times a day, police across the country query the NCIC databases from their patrol cars and their police stations. Using the National Law Enforcement Telecommunications System (NLETS) to access NCIC, the response is essentially instantaneous and is a crucial element both in apprehending wanted persons and officer safety. Whenever an officier pulls over a motorist, the first thing he does before getting out of his patrol car is check the license plate in NCIC. When he returns to his vehicle with the motorist's driver's license and registration, he runs a second NCIC for wanted persons.

It is of utmost importance, however, to understand that this warehouse will simply be that – a warehouse of data. To turn it into information it must be "transformed into knowledge related to a purpose," as stated in the introduction to this paper, and rapidly disseminated to national policymakers, intelligence agencies, the military, and law enforcement agencies.

Considering the volume of this data, this transformation would need to be accomplished electronically using rules defined and developed by the business consideration, i.e., thwarting terrorism. Data mining tools, knowledge management systems, and network communications technologies would be seamlessly combined to integrate the various data, imagery, and analyses at all levels of classification. Analytical profiling tools could be developed to accomplish this end, first using the historical perspective of known cases of terrorism.

Obviously, full access to the security systems of organizations such as the CIA, FBI, INS, DOS, DOD, NSA, and others could not be obtained insofar as such unfettered access could pose severe risks. And, while we in no way minimize the political as well as legal barriers to the sharing of information, the mood of the country and the Congress is ripe to change these attitudinal and legalistic barriers. It is mandatory that basic information be obtained and analyzed in a holistic manner to reasonably expect the ultimate detection and prevention of terrorism.

SHARING DATA SAFELY AND QUICKLY

Of course, the rules surrounding how a source database is accessed and what information is extracted must not jeopardize any assets of the contributing agency. As an example, it is possible that disclosing detailed FBI information about an individual suspect might put that individual, the investigating agent, or the investigation itself in jeopardy. In that instance, the feed from the FBI may simply be a flag to alert other organizations that have reason to interact with the suspect that coordination with the FBI is required. Obviously, security of the system and the automated feeds would need to be extremely high, but all of that is achievable with today's technology.

Once a data warehouse has been created, the next step would then be the systematic analysis of the information available within the repository to identify those characteristics which best describe suspects or suspicious activity. Additional investigations may then be targeted to those suspects resulting in additional information back to the entity through an automated feed.[8]

Building an intelligent repository of "suspects" and the data about them will be no trivial effort. It could take several months, if not years, to analyze all our intelligence needs and build suitable business rules to craft a comprehensive system that fully meets our requirements. The risk here is that it might take too long and our requirements might change even before we get our initial reports. Our suggested approach is therefore based on the following concepts:

Expediency: Look for quick-hit opportunities with a minimum data set that is easy to extract, clean, and standardize across the initial selected agencies. In order to accomplish this in the shortest timeframe feasible, the interconnected system should make maximum use of currently available networks.

Targeted Data Set: The initial data loads will come from a select group of key agencies such as the CIA, FBI, DOD, DOS, and INS to meet specific intelligence goals.

Evolutionary Build: The warehouse design will permit evolutionary growth. After meeting the initial goal, additional capabilities, dimensions, volumes, and business intelligence can be added. Further development could provide feedback to the various entities based on the specific need-to-know of that particular agency.

Cross-Agency Data to Merge Stovepipes: By aggregating information from various agencies, we can develop a fuller picture of the individuals and groups.

Sponsorship: Clearly, such a project will not succeed without commitment at the highest agency levels to determine and extract relevant data from the source systems at these agencies.

Once operational, this data set has a multitude of applications that can be safely and securely put into use through providing inquiry access. Ultimately, it is envisioned that such access could be quite widespread, such as allowing ticketing agents of airlines to determine if a person attempting to purchase a ticket is on a "watch" list and, if so, to notify the appropriate agency immediately. Financial institutions could initiate queries about individuals making large cash transactions. A requirement could be placed on flight schools that they clear individuals attempting to enroll in flight training.

APPLYING THE SOLUTION TO BORDER CONTROL

As noted above, a central repository of information could be quite beneficial in many environments. But one of the first automation efforts should be to assist in controlling the borders of the United States.

How would the principles of intelligence data management outlined above apply in the area of border control? First, we advocate that source data from the Department of State and INS be immediately integrated into the repository so that all agencies involved in granting visas and guarding the border have access to the same data.

We strongly recommend that an effort begin immediately to start collecting a set of biographic and biometric data about every non-immigrant.[9] This data will evolve into an available, reliable source of information for the intelligence and law enforcement communities.

Improving the background checks (to include a positive identity and a criminal history background check) conducted prior to issuing visa identification cards[10] and extending these background checks to everyone wishing to enter the United States (including Canadians, Mexicans, and those countries currently under the Visa Waiver Program) ensures we have access to important data from the start and may prevent known terrorists from ever gaining entrance. For those non-immigrants already in the United States on visas, we must quickly ascertain their status and require, as we used to, that they regularly check in so that we can track their movements in the United States and out of the country. Those non-immigrants who fail to surface immediately will be subject to identity checks just as soon as they do surface. We envision bolstering existing processes with proven technology available now, such that non-immigrants are quickly subject to the process laid out below:

Before Entering the United States

Anyone wishing to gain entry into the United States (tourists, students, employees, and all others) undergoes "universal fingerprinting" at the Department of State (DoS) consulate or other overseas DoS entity. The applicant's fingerprints, photograph, and signature are captured as part of the application process. Everyone wishing to gain entry into the United States is subject to a background check (including both a fingerprint and name check) against a supra-database (including watch list data originating from INS, FBI, and other intelligence agencies). The applicant's biographical and biometric data are stored in a tracking database. The DOS issues a secure identification card (i.e., visa)[11] to applicants who clear the background check – the identification card includes fingerprint data, photo, and signature and is required to gain entry at the U.S. port of entry. (Applicants already in the United States undergo this same application process at INS.)

Upon Entry into the United States

At the U.S. port of entry, the non-immigrant presents his/her identification card, and two of their fingerprints are taken electronically. The two prints provided at the port of entry are compared to both the fingerprint data on the identification card as well as to the fingerprint data stored. If all data matches, the non-immigrant provides his/her U.S. address and is admitted into the United States. The date of entry, port of entry, as well as the U.S. address is captured in the tracking database. If any questions remain after comparing data, the non-immigrant may be turned away or held for further questioning.

While in the United States

While in the United States, the non-immigrant regularly checks in with INS at a local Application Support Center (ASC)[12] and also checks in to report any changes to address, contact, or status information.[13] At each check-in, the ASC employee verifies the non-immigrant's identity against the data provided on the card as well as the tracking database, and updates data in that database. Should non-immigrants fail to check in or fail to depart before their visa date expires (i.e., "overstay"), a trigger automatically adds those non-immigrants to the watch list database.

Visitors, typically in the United States for 90 days or less, would be required to check in every 30 days. Students, for whom academic and vocational institutions track student progress, would be required to maintain class records and check in upon enrollment, every 90 days, and upon graduation or otherwise leaving school. Educational institutions also report students' enrollment and departures to INS. Should a student fail to report a change subsequently reported by an educational institution, they are added to the watch list database. Employees check in upon being hired, every 120 days, and upon changing employers. Employers also report hires and departures of non-immigrants. Should an employee fail to report a change subsequently reported by an employer, he/she is added to the watch list database.

Upon Departure from the United States

The non-immigrant presents his/her identification card upon departure from the United States. The non-immigrant's identity is again verified and his/her departure date, port of entry, and forwarding address are posted in the tracking database.

INTEGRATION IS IMPERATIVE

The foregoing has provided an overview approach to the issue of detection of known or suspected terrorists through the rapid and efficient deployment of technology. Once operational, this technology could then be made available to innumerable agencies, departments and private enterprises on a limited need-to-know basis, protecting our intelligence infrastructure while at the same time providing comprehensive, meaningful information to those people making decisions on both a strategic and tactical level. At a minimum, the integration of those systems necessary to make informed decisions about those who cross our borders, either legally or illegally, is imperative.

ENDNOTES

1 Our premise is that at some point, additional sources and methods may be required to obtain more information, but, until a comprehensive view of the available data is consolidated and analyzed, the extent of those resources is not known.

2 The United States Bureau of Prison population at the end of September 1999 was 133,689, with illegal aliens comprising 29.1 percent, or 38,903, of those incarcerated. In 1999, the nation's jails held an additional 24,000 criminal aliens out of a total jail population of 605,943, or 5 percent of the total.

3 Of the 525 million, 115 million crossed the northern land border, 319 million crossed the southern land border, and 91 million were at air and seaports.

4 Basically, although the INS inspector has the authority to refer individuals crossing the borders for secondary inspection, only a small percentage of the total are subjected to this more thorough inspection process.

5 Testimony of Michael D. Cronin, Acting Associate Commissioner Programs, Immigration, and Naturalization Service, Regarding Non-Immigrant Overstays before the House Judiciary Committee, Subcommittee on Immigration and Claims, Thursday, March 18, 1999.

6 Biometric technology such as retinal scans, facial mapping, and digital fingerprinting has progressed dramatically in the past decade and is viewed as an integral part of the ultimate solution.

7 In the sake of expediency, it is recommended that rather than attempting to provide interaction with the roughly 40 separate government entities possessing intelligence information, a critical sub-set of these be identified and integrated as the first steps. After this first iteration is brought up and proven successful, integration with other entities could then be phased in.

8 Ultimately, it is highly probable that information fed back to the portal database would prove useful in automating feeds back to the contributing agencies. For instance, it is possible that the occurrence of a person who is the subject of an investigation attempting to purchase an airline ticket would automatically feed back to the agency performing the investigation.

9   INS could immediately begin capturing data (two prints, photos, and biographical information) utilizing its current IDENT system at borders and ports of entry on a broader base of non-immigrants. This would require increasing capacity throughout the system.

10 Immigrants, or those individuals applying for legal permanent residence in the United States, as well as legal permanent residents applying for citizenship, are currently subject to background checks.

11 The process to provide this identification card could be similar in nature to the provision of the Border Crossing Card used currently for Mexicans crossing into the United States on a recurring basis.

12 Application Support Centers are community-based INS offices that were established primarily in metropolitan areas with large known applicant populations. These facilities were designed to provide convenient access (0 to 25 miles) to fingerprinting services for 92 percent of the INS's customers. ASCs act as full-service fingerprint locations that are capable of processing all applicants who require fingerprints to receive an INS benefit. Recently, some ASCs have begun to also capture applicants' digital photographs and signatures in addition to fingerprints for certain benefits.

13 It seems that INS could simply revive a version of the 1940 Alien Registration Act to require foreigners to periodically report to an INS office.

INSTITUTIONAL ISSUES IN BIODEFENSE

Tara O'Toole

The October 2001 anthrax attacks may have given Americans the wrong idea about bioweapons and bioterrorism. As disruptive as the attacks were to certain workplaces – including the U.S. Senate and the Postal Service – in the end, only 18 people were diagnosed with anthrax, and only five died. In comparison with the some of the dire bioterrorism scenarios that had been painted, some might even find October's events reassuring.

Just the opposite is the case. The nation's response to the attacks revealed inadequacies in our medical and public health systems that would have been truly devastating in the face of a larger attack. I will agree that biological weapons are a growing threat to the national community. What's more, bioweapons are a *strategic* threat – meaning one that could destroy fundamental institutions and democratic systems.

There is much we can do to mitigate the consequences of a biological weapons attack. There is also a lot that can be done to help prevent research and development in biological weapons. But such mitigative and preventive actions are going to require significant institutional changes as well as technological advances. Creating the appropriate "socio-technical systems," as professor Louise Comfort of the University of Pittsburgh has put it, is one of the major challenges of our generation.

BIOWEAPONS ARE A STRATEGIC THREAT

Before the needed new systems can be created, it is important to understand the magnitude and nature of the bioweapons threat. In its report "New World Coming: American Security in the 21st Century," the Hart-Rudman Commission concluded that biological weapons are going to be one of the biggest security threats facing the United States in the coming years. The commission's September 1999 report stated:

> [F]or many years to come Americans will become increasingly less secure, and much less secure than they now believe themselves to be. … While conventional conflicts will still be possible, the most serious threat to our security may consist of unannounced attacks on American cities by sub-national groups using genetically engineered pathogens.

Biological weapons, even in crude forms, have the potential to inflict horrible suffering and death on a large scale. In this age of globalization, an attack on U.S. citizens could quickly become a worldwide epidemic.

Lethality

Biological weapons can be extremely lethal. A 1993 Congressional Office of Technology Assessment study estimated that 100 kilograms of anthrax released upwind of Washington, D.C., under ideal metrological conditions would have approximately the same lethality as a 1-megaton hydrogen bomb dropped on that city. Each could kill millions.

The impact of an epidemic such as one caused by a bioterrorist attack can be illustrated by a 1972 smallpox outbreak in Yugoslavia. Vaccination with roadside checkpoints was mandated for the entire population of 20 million; 10,000 contacts of the original smallpox cases were held in hotels surrounded by barbed wire and military guard; population movement was restricted and public meetings prohibited; and borders with neighboring countries were completely closed – and this was in a setting of universal, mandatory vaccination. This outbreak (175 cases with 35 deaths) was considered small.

The letter Senator Tom Daschle received contained only 2 grams – almost too little to feel in an envelope – of highly powderized anthrax. Those 2 grams were the equivalent of 2 *million* lethal doses, had they been distributed perfectly. It is difficult for people to wrap their minds around the notion of that much lethality packed in such a seemingly benign and small package. But in fact, biological weapons are quite capable of bringing the country past the "point of non-recovery," as Adm. Stansfield Turner, former director of the U.S. Central Intelligence Agency, called it. The economic and social disruption resulting from a large bioweapons attack could conceivably generate sufficient fear and urgency to threaten fundamental democratic principles, and could undermine confidence in government.

Accessible, Cheap, Easily Hidden

A second reason biological weapons are a strategic threat is that the materials needed to build them are accessible, cheap, and easily hidden. The Department of Defense did an experiment a few years ago: three men, none of whom had special expertise in bioweapons, with a budget of $250,000, made a very good batch of anthrax stimulant using equipment bought off the Internet. It is wrong to allege, as the press did, that making highly purified, "weaponized" anthrax is beyond the reach of anyone outside of a state-sponsored bioweapons program. It's actually relatively simple, and it has been done.

This fermenter from the Al Hakan plant outside Baghdad was used to produce anthrax. One fermenter contains 1,500 liters. When concentrated, the solution in this fermenter contains enough lethal doses to kill everyone on the planet. Yet the fermenter itself is a perfectly legitimate piece of equipment and easy to obtain. You can wash it out, put it on a truck, and move it around. It is much easier to hide than is, for example, a uranium-enrichment plant needed to make nuclear weapons-grade uranium. Biological weapons are known as the "poor man's atomic bomb" for a reason: compared to missiles or nukes, they are cheap to build, and you can get whatever you need on the market.

The State Department estimates that at least 12 countries have ongoing offensive biological weapons programs, including all of those on its list of state sponsors of terrorism.

Appeal of Asymmetric Weapons

Biological weapons can be built without the support of a nation-state or the infrastructure of a highly technologically advanced society. These characteristics make them very appealing as so-called "asymmetric threats." Bioweapons enable attacks on America without having to confront the tremendous power of the U.S. military.

It is generally agreed that overt use of a biological weapon by a nation-state is unlikely because of the severe retribution that would ensue if the attacker were identified. Retribution is less of a deterrent for extremist groups intent on inflicting large numbers of casualties. Both Osama bin Laden's group and the Japanese religious cult Aum Shinrikyo have used or threatened to use biological weapons – the latter made several attempts to release anthrax in downtown Tokyo before the 1995 serum gas attack in that city's subway.

As former Senator Sam Nunn has said, it's much more likely that would-be terrorists bent on using a weapon of mass destruction would try something that doesn't come with "a return address." A ballistic missile coming across the Pacific is arguably much less likely than an attack using an atomic bomb in a suitcase or a biological weapon and before October 2001, who ever would have thought of envelopes as a weapons delivery system?

GROWING POWER OF BIOSCIENCE AND ITS "DARK SIDE"

A fundamental reason biological weapons constitute such an important strategic threat has to do with their linkage to the trajectory of biological science in the 21st century. The world is entering the age of Big Biology. The growing power to manipulate the viruses and bacteria that have plagued humankind through history can be applied toward both beneficent and evil ends. Nuclear physics is not the only science with a dark side.

Our understanding of the life sciences is advancing at an unprecedented pace, which is sure to bring fantastic opportunities for prevention and treatment of disease and progress in agricultural techniques. As a consequence of the platform built by the advances in engineering and computational sciences in the 20th century, biologists can now generate enormous amounts of information very quickly. Information about bioscience is widely disseminated across the globe and is used for many, many purposes. Propelled by international corporations with high profit margins, these advances are producing products for which there is an avid appetite.

But advances in bioscience and biotechnology may also increase the potential power and diversity of biological weapons. Every time we gain in understanding how virulence is achieved by a particular bacteria or virus or what causes antibiotic resistance, we are learning how we could make a better vaccine or a more effective treatment. That same knowledge, however, can be used to *make* a more virulent bug or an antibiotic-resistant germ. We are also developing techniques to potentially alter the way microorganisms behave, so that infections typically transmitted only through oral-fecal contact might be rendered contagious via respiratory contact, for example.

The dual-use capacity of biological research is very worrisome. While you can easily tell the difference between the technologies used to build a nuclear power plant and those required to create a nuclear weapon, the distinction between "good" biology and dark biology hinges on its application and intent to a degree that no other technology really has.

The Soviet biological weapons program, which Brezhnev began secretly in the 1970s right after the USSR signed the biological weapons convention, had made a lot of progress before the West realized in 1991 what was going on. And we realized what was happening only through high-level defectors.

By the 1980s or so, the Soviets had not only made *ton* quantities of smallpox, anthrax, and plague, all in weaponized form, they were also experimenting with viral weapons. They were alleged to have been working on hybridizing the Marburg virus, which is an Ebola-like hemorrhagic fever virus. They were also working on antibiotic-resistant weapons. We know they created antibiotic-resistant plague. And they were beginning to explore the use of smaller molecules (such as peptides) as weapons to induce mood changes.

Since the end of the Cold War, much of the *Biopreparat* program has been dismantled. But we don't know what's happened to the 30,000 scientists who once worked in the Soviet bioweapons program; there is concern that some may have gone to Iran, Iraq, or North Korea. And we have no idea what happened to the black military programs. We don't know where the cultures or the culture recipes for the Soviet bioweapons stocks are, or whether they might have found their way into the hands of rogue states or terrorist groups.

There are tens of thousands of highly trained bioscientists all around the globe. This is very different from the situation that pertained in 1945, when most of the 100 scientists who knew anything about nuclear fission were all behind barbed wire on a mesa in Los Alamos.

GLOBALIZATION AND VULNERABILITY TO INFECTIOUS DISEASE

There is another reason to worry about biological weapons and the epidemics they cause: the consequences of interconnectedness and globalization.

Tens of millions of people live in mega-cities in conditions that include poor sanitation, poor nutrition, lack of clean water, and close proximity to their animals. These are perfect breeding grounds for pathogens, whose spread to far corners of the world is facilitated by global commerce and rapid travel. In about 24 hours, you can cross to the other side of the planet. During the pandemic flu outbreak in 1918 it took six weeks to do this – but that was the age of trolley cars and steamships.

Commercialization and population pressures are driving human activity into once remote ecosystems, where we come into contact with things like Ebola and HIV. We now rely on huge food interconnected supply chains that make it very difficult to detect or contain contamination. One hamburger contains parts from about 100 cows that come from feedlots containing some 100,000 animals. Figuring out exactly where the E-coli in a particular hamburger came from is virtually impossible.

Last year's foot-and-mouth disease outbreak in Great Britain taught us that we are still very vulnerable to infectious diseases. As we move into the era when more and more of the pathogens we are confronting are antibiotic-resistant, we're going to realize anew the devastation these sorts of illnesses cause in the world.

ATTACKS HIGHLIGHTED INSTITUTIONAL WEAKNESSES

The consequences of biological weapons attacks are very different from the consequences of other forms of catastrophic terrorism. An epidemic is not a "lights-and-sirens" event. The medical and public health communities will be at the core of any response to bioterrorism, and our way out of the peril we are in depends very intimately on the ability to use our scientific prowess to create an effective biodefense capability.

Currently, the medical, public health, and bioresearch communities face several serious problems. The institutional capacities of American health care and public health systems are inadequate to manage a mass-casualty event. Bioscience talent is not engaged in biodefense. Political leaders are unfamiliar with key issues. Responding to a large bioterrorist attack will inevitably engage a welter of inter-institutional issues that have to do with coordination, not just of different organizations, but of different organizational cultures on levels that range from local governments and universities all the way up to federal, national, and international levels.

The anthrax attacks of October 2001 are not the story of biological weapons. They are not even the *prologue* to the story of biological weapons. There were only 18 confirmed cases of anthrax – 11 inhalational and seven cutaneous. People in four states and the District of Columbia were affected; five people died. Despite their small number, however, the anthrax cases do offer some useful illustrations of the deficiencies of our current system – made all the more alarming by the fact that the number of cases was in no way comparable to the potential threat.

INADEQUATE DATA, INFORMATION FLOW

The first deficiency that became apparent in the 2001 anthrax attacks is that decision-makers lacked situational awareness – they had great difficulty obtaining enough information to understand what was going on. HHS Secretary Tommy Thompson forfeited a lot of credibility with his early announcement that the index case in Florida was an isolated case, possibly attributable to the victim drinking contaminated water during a camping trip, and with his subsequent assertion to a Senate committee that the public health system was "fully prepared" to deal with any bioterrorist attack. This was not simply an instance of inadequate leadership by an individual. For weeks, members of the media as well as local public health officials and clinicians had great difficulty accessing the federal government's analysis of or recommendations about the anthrax threat. The precise reasons for this protracted dearth of information remain unclear.

It was also the case that existing data was not always effectively applied or accurately interpreted by health officials or the media and public. For example, it was widely reported in the media and by public health officials that inhalation of at least 10,000 anthrax spores was nec-

essary to infect an individual. Anyone familiar with the scientific literature on anthrax realized this was a significant misinterpretation; the
data show that far fewer spores can infect at least some subjects. Also,
Canadian Defense Forces study released in September 2001 provided
important information about how far and fast an anthrax simulant pow-
der contained in envelopes was likely to spread in a room. Yet it was
weeks before the CDC recognized this information.

Perhaps one of the most significant institutional failures in the anthrax response was the lack of any process or system for identifying and
working through the many novel and complex "science questions,"
which emerged as the attacks and subsequent interventions proceeded.
It is not reasonable to expect those who are in the midst of managing
field operations during a crisis to also identify and solve complicated
technical issues. HHS was very slow to locate or muster the
multidisciplinary expertise required to address the diverse technical issues that arose. Although the CDC initiated a number of conference
calls and held some meetings of outside experts to discuss specific issues, these were usually arranged at the last minute and poorly organized. Scientists from universities and industry who believed they had
directly relevant information to offer claimed – as they has during the
West Nile Virus outbreak of 1999 – that they could not get the attention
of public health decision-makers.

MEDICAL SYSTEM VULNERABILITIES

Although only 18 cases of anthrax were confirmed in 2001, the anthrax mailings imposed significant stress on the medical system in the
cities and towns associated with the attacks. For example, at the hospital in northern Virginia that cared for two of the postal workers with
anthrax, the usual number of emergency room visits doubled in the
days following the attacks. Any highly visible disease outbreak typically
causes many anxious patients to seek care and reassurance from health
care providers. This would certainly be the case in a large bioterrorist
attack – especially since the early symptoms of the most likely
bioweapons pathogens closely resemble the symptoms of common, benign illnesses.

Unfortunately, the U.S. health care system has very little capacity to
respond to sudden surges in patient demand. The financial pressures on
hospitals and health care organizations have caused these institutions
to cut staff, eliminate emergency rooms, and to apply just-in-time sup-

ply models to management of everything from nurses to pharmaceuticals. There is no hospital or geographically contiguous collection of hospitals in the country that could cope with 1,000 patients suddenly needing advanced medical care.

Moreover, the bioterrorism response planning carried out in some cities during the past few years through the Nunn Lugar Domenici Domestic Preparedness Programs, has, for the most part, not included hospitals. The hospitals claim that their busy personnel cannot be spared to participate in these training programs and exercises. The result is that few municipalities have any community-wide plans for dealing with the medical care aspects of large-scale disasters.

There are no quick fixes to the problems associated with mass-casualty care in our overburdened health care system. Thirty percent of all U.S. hospitals are in the red; half of all academic medical centers are losing money.

Hospitals today are usually full to overflowing and have little capacity to deal with even a small, sudden surge of patients, such as that brought on by a typical influenza season. Leaders in Congress and the executive branch have not convinced hospital leaders that bioterrorism represents a serious national security threat, or that the medical care system is expected to play a significant response role, should an attack occur. Nor has the government instituted any mandates or provided any incentives that would encourage hospitals to divert scarce and precious resources toward bioterrorism preparation and planning. As a result, hospitals are not part of the community-wide response. Getting them in the game is going to be a real challenge.

PUBLIC HEALTH VULNERABILITIES

The nation's public health system, like the health care delivery system, lacks the capacity necessary to respond to a surge in demand for services. Public health has been underfunded and understaffed for decades. Health departments in the cities and states affected by the anthrax attacks had to struggle mightily to cope with the demands of what turned out to be only 18 confirmed cases of anthrax.

CDC laboratory personnel were literally living in the lab, trying to keep up with the demand for diagnostic tests, getting only catnaps for days on end. In Maryland, the state laboratory was overwhelmed by the over 2,000 instances of "suspicious powders" needing analysis. In states where anthrax cases surfaced, local health officials did little else but "all anthrax all the time." Personnel from other departments were called in to analyze reports of emergency room visits, to man public hot-lines, and to respond to physician inquiries. This diversion of resources was unfunded and unsustainable.

If 18 cases of anthrax taxed our public health system to this extent, what can we expect from a large attack involving thousands of victims? Most of the public health officials pulled into duty had no training in bioterrorism. Most states and cities improvised as they sought ways to meet the demand. With more than 30 states now enduring hiring freezes in response to the economic downturn, even current response capacity may be eroded.

It is essential that we find ways to enable health departments at the federal, state, and local levels to attract and hire more people and to provide them with high-quality training. It could be especially important to find ways to import physicians with specialty backgrounds in infectious disease, epidemiology, and emergency medicine into public health.

The 8,000 local, state, city, and federal public health agencies in this country do not really constitute a "system." There is little connectivity among these organizations. Half of the local public health departments do not have access to the Internet. This was reflected in the difficulty local health departments had getting timely information from CDC during the anthrax attacks. Federal guidance sometimes took days to reach local health officials, many of whom were forced to rely on media for updates on events.

Effective management of an epidemic is a complex and difficult task, often compounded by high levels of public anxiety and concomitant interruptions in critical services such as transportation. American physicians and public health practitioners have limited experience in such contexts. Few professionals have had any experience with many of the diseases identified as potentially dangerous biological weapons such as Ebola virus or anthrax.

Much might be gained from the development of an international surveillance network of epidemiologists and physicians, prepared to quickly investigate and intervene in outbreaks of infectious disease epidemics throughout the world. In the modern world, epidemics, especially of contagious disease, are not simply national problems; they are potential threats to international security.

ROBUST R&D PROGRAM FOR BIODEFENSE: "BIO APOLLO"

At present, the great advantage in bioweaponry belongs to the aggressor. By leveraging existing investments already being made by the private sector, the U.S. government could spur the creation of new strategies for coping with bioweapons and infectious disease generally. Over the next few years, developments in the life sciences could create critically useful vaccines and medicines that could make bioweapons far less menacing and less likely to be used. Asking the Federal Emergency Management Agency to coordinate a bioterrorism response armed only with the vaccines and antimicrobial drugs currently available is tantamount to asking firefighters to battle a 12-alarm blaze without water or foam.

Turning the advantage in biological weapons to the defense will require a major investment in R&D. This should be a joint effort undertaken by the Defense Department and the Department of Health and Human Services.

In the near term, biodefense R&D should focus on developing better vaccines and medicines and diagnostic capabilities. In the longer term, we must learn enough about the immune system to enable us to very rapidly respond to a wide variety of possible biological agents, including bioengineered weapons. If we do that, in the process we will inevitably learn a lot more about many infectious diseases, including drug-resistant TB, malaria, and HIV. Infectious diseases now cause half of the premature mortality in the developing world. According to the National Intelligence Council, this burden of infectious disease may stand in the way of some nations making the transition to democracy. Should we learn enough to eliminate or effectively treat these scourges of the developing world, we could arguably diminish some the causes of terrorism at their root.

CONTROLLING THE DARK SIDE OF BIOSCIENCE

The advances in infrastructure, system-building, and technology outlined above will prepare this nation and the international community to better respond to bioweapons attacks. But we won't be truly secure until we can also prevent such attacks in the first place. To do this, we need a completely new approach to arms control, and it must relate to the way we do biological science.

Conventional arms control approaches, such as mutual deterrence, cannot be relied upon to deter bioterrorism because, as we have seen with the anthrax attacks, it is difficult to assign attribution for such attacks. Because individuals can build and wield biological weapons, international treaties are not sufficient to control this threat. Traditional government regulations, such as those that would require special security measures for work with specified "select agent" pathogens, cannot control weapons development from bacteria and viruses that are naturally available, or prevent the potentially malignant applications of research pursued in good faith for beneficent purposes.

A new framework of scientific self-governance is needed to cope with the growing power of biological knowledge. The new framework will likely involve training and accreditation to increase researchers' awareness of biosecurity issues, monitoring of critical databases, new protocols for reviewing and publishing findings and methods, and possibly scientific review boards for especially problematic issues. Scientists must be at the heart of any new systems designed to control this power.

It is imperative to build a universal consensus, particularly among scientists, that the development, production, or dissemination of biological weapons by any persons, laboratories, or governments would be regarded by the world community as one of the most serious of all crimes.

Samuel Huntington wrote in *The Clash of Civilizations*:

The American political genius is manifest not in our ideas but in our institutions. The greatest need is not so much the creation of more liberal institutions as the successful defense of those which already exist.

The Hart-Rudman Commission was right in its analysis that the biggest threat facing us is the disparity between advances in biotechnology and our ability to develop systems that can effectively and responsibly manage them. To deal with the threats of bioterrorism, we catalyze an evolutionary jump in the medical, public health, and bioresearch systems of the present day. It will be one of the great tasks of our generation to get there.

REFERENCES

Bass, Robert R. and Georges C. Benjamin. *The Maryland Strategic Plan to Improve the Health and Medical Response to Terrorism.* Baltimore, MD: Maryland Institute for Emergency Medical Services Systems, February 2000.

Gannon, John C. *"The Global Infectious Disease Threat and Its Implications for the United States." The Global Infectious Disease. Jan. 2000 NIE99-17D*, http://www.odci.gov/cia/publications/nie/report/nie99-17d.html.

Jernigan, John A., David S. Stephens, David A. Ashford, et al. "Bioterrorism-Related Inhalational Anthrax: The First 10 Cases Reported in the United States." *Emerging Infectious Diseases.* 2001 Nov-Dec; 7 (6): 933-944.

Moodie, Michael and William J. Taylor Jr. 2000. *Contagion and Conflict: Health as a Global Security Challenge.* Washington, D.C.: Center for Strategic and International Studies.

Office of the Under Secretary of Defense For Acquisition, Technology, and Logistics. *Defense Against Biological Weapons: Leveraging Advances in Biotechnology and Medical Informatics to Improve Homeland Biodefense Capabilities.* Oct. 2001. Washington, D.C. Vol. 5.

Smithson, Amy E. and Leslie-Anne Levy. *Ataxia: The Chemical and Biological Terrorism Threat and the U.S. Response.* 2000. Washington, D.C.: The Henry L. Stimson Center. Report No. 35.

The United States Commission on National Security/21st Century. *Road Map for National Security: Imperative for Change.* Feb. 2001. www.nssg.gov.

U.S. Congress, Office of Technology Assessment. *Technologies Underlying Weapons of Mass Destruction. OTA-BP-ISC-115* (Washington, D.C.: U.S. Government Printing Office, December 1993).

GOVERNANCE UNDER FIRE: ORGANIZATIONAL FRAGILITY IN COMPLEX SYSTEMS

Louise K. Comfort

POLICY PROBLEM

Maintaining public security is the quintessential function of government. The events of September 11, 2001, provided an extraordinary test of existing governmental policy and practice. While the response to these events demonstrated remarkable courage by public agencies and personnel, winning national recognition for their effort and dedication, the fact that the events occurred and the scope of the losses endured compel us to re-examine the concepts, design, and context for action of public agencies that are legally responsible for the protection of life and property. This is not a simple task, and requires a fresh look at some long-held assumptions about governmental operations in complex environments.

Existing administrative procedures generally assume a stable, organizational environment with regular procedures operating under normal conditions with time to plan actions, allocate resources and attention, and identify and correct errors before they cause failure. Sudden, threatening events require a rapid shift in perspective, a capacity to absorb damaging information, the mental agility to re-assess the situation in light of changing events, and an ability to formulate new strategies of action in uncertain environments. The difference in decision processes between stable and dynamic operating environments has been noted by theorists in cognitive psychology (Weick 1995; 2001), business (McKelvey 1999), and military affairs (Alberts, Gartska, and Stein 1999), but has drawn less attention in the field of public administration and policy. The events of September 11 no longer allow the luxury of ignoring the substantive difference in decision processes for public agencies operating in dynamic environments or failing to consider the interaction between organizational and technical structures that facilitate the rapid assessment of risk and mobilization of response vital to maintain public security.

Demands placed upon decision-makers in urgent, stressful environments are cognitive, physical, emotional, organizational, and cultural (Dror 1986; Flin 1996). These demands exceed human capacity to function effectively under standard administrative procedures. The rational model of listing all alternatives for action, weighing the costs and benefits of each alternative, and choosing among them based on careful calculation simply takes too long for most experienced emergency personnel facing an urgent, dynamic situation. More damning, it is almost always wrong as information and conditions change rapidly in an evolving, interdependent set of events. Rather, most experienced personnel rely upon rapid assessment of the situation, matching it mentally against a repertoire of similar conditions they have seen before, and creating a strategy of plausible action from the resources available to them. Gary Klein (1993), a theorist of naturalistic decision-making, terms this process "recognition primed decision-making." Karl Weick (1995), a psychologist, refers to the process of interpreting rapidly changing events as a basis for action as "sensemaking." These processes rely largely on mental models of effective operations in familiar conditions and the capacity to detect errors at the margins. But even these methods are limited when decision-makers face unimaginable events, such as the deliberate transformation of commercial airliners into destructive missiles. Herbert Simon (1981), in his classic book, *The Sciences of the Artificial*, stated, "we can only create what we already know." The challenge lies in recognizing the preliminary indicators of risk and associating them in an understandable pattern of threat before disaster occurs.

The events of September 11 revealed that some governmental operations proved very effective, while others suffered from serious failures. In a classic "after-action review," it is imperative to ask tough questions. At what point do interorganizational operations fail? What are the limits of existing governmental systems? What changes can be made to strengthen governmental performance under threat? How can we learn from this sobering experience?

ORGANIZATIONAL FRAGILITY CURVES

In the field of engineering, the concept of a fragility curve implies that a building, as an engineered structure, does not fail all at once, but is subject to strains and stresses that cumulate until it reaches a point where it loses structural viability and collapses (Chopra and Goel 1999). Organizational systems, as socially designed structures, are similarly subject to stresses and strains that cumulate until they reach a point where the system loses viability and collapses, or is no longer able to function effectively. The materials for the two types of systems differ. Engineered buildings are made of steel, concrete, bricks, and mortar and result in a physical construction at a given geographical location. Organizations, as "artificial constructs" designed by social architects, consist of policies, procedures, information, resources, and human problem-solving capacity (Simon 1981). Organizational systems, in contrast to engineered structures, operate largely within domains of human communication and coordination and need not be limited by physical location. Their primary resource is information that enables multiple members to coordinate their actions to achieve a stated goal, deliver a desired service, or produce a preferred outcome. Their most distinctive characteristic is that, designed and operated by human managers, they also have the capacity to learn and adapt to new situations (Argryis and Schon 1996; Axelrod 1997). The goal of maintaining operational performance under varying conditions, however, is the same for both types of systems.

In studies of engineered buildings, a great deal of attention, thought, and research has focused on how buildings fail, under what conditions, triggered by what mechanisms, and at what critical points in their design under different degrees of stress. For example, earthquake engineers, using massive "shake tables," test various construction designs with different materials to determine which perform better under varying degrees of stress. Using careful measures of tensile strength, they calculate the "fragility curve" of a building to determine the type and degree of stress it can withstand and the points at which it will fail (Casciati and Faravelli 1991). Their intent is to learn how and where to reinforce vulnerable points in the building to absorb probable levels of stress from environmental changes.

In governance, relatively little attention has focused on developing organizational capacity for adaptation to changing environments, and almost no attention has been given to the measurement of an interorganizational system's capacity to function under severe threat. At present, there is no viable measure of organizational fragility curves for organizations performing under stress.

The events of September 11, 2001, offer a striking opportunity to study both types of fragility. The engineered structures of the World Trade Center collapsed under the intense heat of 2,000 degrees from the jet-fueled fires. Steel loses its integrity at 1,500 degrees, and as the fires burned, the buildings failed in a stunning cloud of ash and debris. Similarly, organizational structures designed to protect security also failed under the incomprehensible threat of suicide aircraft bombers. The security checks at Logan Airport in Boston, Dulles, and Newark Airports did not detect the box cutters and knives used by the hijackers to wrest control of the planes from crews and to subdue the passengers. More soberly, sensemaking failed on the flights from Boston and Dulles as crews and passengers followed previous procedures for coping with hijackers in expecting to negotiate a release from danger, without detecting the hijackers' true intent. In each instance, the crews and passengers on these planes faced unimaginable events. They did not recognize the risk and were unable to act to avert danger.

Other incidents on this fateful Tuesday indicate similar failures of organizational sensemaking in the face of unrecognized danger. The loss of 343 personnel from the New York City Fire Department followed from standard departmental procedures to establish their command post close to the fireground to serve as their base of operations (Fritsch 2001; Perez-Pena 2001). The location of the Emergency Medical Services (EMS) triage station under the bridge between the towers would ordinarily have offered welcome shelter to this critical operation. But without knowledge of the structural vulnerability of the buildings, the entire EMS station was lost when the tower collapsed onto the bridge.

The sobering events of 9-11 provide an unusual opportunity to assess the fragility of the interorganizational systems involved in protecting public safety. These events revealed dramatic failure in governmental systems, but also a remarkable capacity to regroup, reorganize, and re-design workable strategies for previously unimaginable circumstances as the sequence of events evolved. The extraordinary actions of the passengers aboard Flight #93 from Newark illustrate the human capacity to accept new information and adapt to a newly recognized threatening situation. After learning that two other hijacked planes had crashed into the World Trade Center via cell phone conversations with family and friends, the passengers acted to challenge the hijackers on their plane, bringing it down in a Pennsylvania field without reaching its intended target, likely in Washington, D.C. Assessing these events carefully may lead to methods of calibrating interorganizational strain and identifying points of potential reinforcement in interorganizational systems that will allow them to withstand severe threats to public safety and adapt to suddenly altered or rapidly changing conditions and urgent demands more effectively.

RESPONSE OPERATIONS FOLLOWING THE SEPTEMBER 11 ATTACKS: AN INTERORGANIZATIONAL SYSTEM

The disaster response process (Federal Emergency Management Agency 1999) in the United States has been developed largely in response to natural disasters: earthquakes, hurricanes, floods, fires, tornadoes, and severe winter storms. It has been honed in practice, particularly in the vulnerable states of California, Florida, and Texas, but every state in the union has been affected by disaster. Conceptually, the process moves from the local community, where the event occurs, to ever-widening circles of assistance and resources. It is a step-wise process where the local municipality must first exhaust its resources before it can declare an emergency and request assistance from the county, the next jurisdictional level. The county responds, exhausts its resources, declares an emergency, and appeals to the state for assistance. The state in turn repeats the process, requesting assistance from the federal government. Each level of appeal must be accompanied by a formal assessment of risk and a demonstration of exhausted resources before the next jurisdictional level accepts it, and resources are then allocated to the lower levels of operation. The assumption is that the federal government will be the responding agency of last resort. But this process is exactly the kind of linear, rational procedure that often does not fit the dynamic conditions in which disaster is occurring. It is designed primarily to track the money and materials that are expended in disaster operations and to compensate jurisdictions and victims for losses already incurred, rather than to provide information or resources needed to reduce risk or anticipate the impact of damaging events upon communities.

SHARED RISK

The threat of a terrorist attack is similar to the threat of earthquakes, hurricanes, floods, and fires in that it represents public risk. That is, the risk is shared by all members of the community, whether they contributed to the circumstances that led to its occurrence or not (Comfort 1999). Consequently, actions taken by any one member may increase or reduce the risk for all other members in the community. The responsibility for mitigation of risk is also shared. In this environment of shared risk and responsibility, the critical function is communication and the capacity to access, store, transmit, receive, and comprehend information in real time as events are unfolding. This function is a socio-technical function, dependent upon the technical infrastructure of communications as well as the procedures and policies of organizations and the cognitive functions of individuals who receive and act (or fail to act) on the content of the information transmitted.

The concept of shared risk is critical to effective emergency management. It means that a community's capacity to mitigate risk and respond to damaging incidents when they occur depends upon its ability to assess its own vulnerabilities, monitor its own performance, and mobilize resources in response to threat. The classic mechanisms of coping with threat have included denial, resistance, flight, or the creation of a new system that includes the threat as an interacting component. It is this last option that offers the most promise for rethinking governmental strategies for coping with terrorism.

Creating an intergovernmental system that acknowledges the threat of terrorism, ill-defined and uncertain in its timing and location, means reviewing carefully the fragility of existing governmental systems that are intended to protect the citizenry from destructive events. Since the primary characteristic of a terrorist act is surprise, and its major targets include civilian populations, the traditional strategies of military defense are all but irrelevant. The major burden in the defense of communities against terrorist attacks will necessarily be borne by civilian emergency response agencies at the local level: police, fire, and emergency medical services, coupled with a careful monitoring by the public and private owners of the interdependent infrastructure systems that serve large numbers of people: communications, electrical power, transportation, water, gas, and sewage distribution systems. Agencies at the local level currently have the least access to resources, training, and capacity to make rapid assessments of risk and build rapidly evolving response systems to reduce or contain threatening events. Enabling these agencies to share information about potentially threatening conditions, inconsistent indicators, or available resources represents a first step toward building an informed community that is able to adapt quickly to changing conditions. It must necessarily be an interorganizational system, and as the threat escalates or widens, it becomes inter-jurisdictional and inter-disciplinary as well.

The events of September 11 illustrated vividly the interorganizational, interjurisdictional, interdisciplinary characteristics of response to terrorism. When the two flights from Boston struck the World Trade Center Towers in lower Manhattan, the incidents occurred within the jurisdiction of New York City, and local fire, police, and emergency medical services immediately responded to the scene. Within the hour, when the flight from Dulles struck the Pentagon, the federal government itself was attacked, and the reality of the terrorist intent became clear. The Federal Emergency Response Plan was not officially invoked, but the training and prior experience of responsible personnel in the federal agencies enabled them to activate their emergency operations centers to adapt quickly to the unfolding events and respond with immediate strategies of assistance to the local agencies in both New York City and Arlington County at the Pentagon site. At both locations, personnel from federal agencies worked directly with local city and county agencies in organizing the response. At both sites, prior contacts and experienced personnel facilitated direct communication between federal and local agencies and enabled the response operations to evolve much more quickly and smoothly than expected, if standard administrative procedures would have been followed. A small group of personnel from key agencies with shared experience recognized the requirements of the situation and were able to adapt quickly to the urgent conditions.

COMPLEX ADAPTIVE SYSTEMS IN DISASTER ENVIRONMENTS

The capacity to adapt to new information and reallocate resources and action accordingly is termed "self organization" in the literature of complex adaptive systems. Stuart Kauffman (1993), a biologist, argued that all systems operate on a continuum between chaos and order, with systems at either end of the continuum moving toward the center. At the center, there is a narrow region termed the "edge of chaos," where there is sufficient order to hold and exchange information, but sufficient flexibility to adapt to a changing environment. At the "edge of chaos," organizations are able to adapt most successfully to changing demands from the environment. Kauffman called this process "self organization," as the change in behavior is initiated by the actor, not imposed by any external force or directive.

This capacity to learn from incoming information in a dynamic environment alters significantly the operating context of organizations responding to threat. It is dependent upon access to information and the range and quality of the information available to operations personnel. Just as the use of cell phones enabled passengers on Flight #93 to learn of the plane crashes at the World Trade Center and to reassess the actions of the hijackers on their own flight, this capacity can be enhanced by a technical infrastructure that establishes contact and communication with a wider range of sources of information and support to organizational personnel. Simultaneously, this capacity can be limited when the technical information infrastructure fails, and vital communications cannot be made.

Viewing organizations as socio-technical systems, dependent upon communications to achieve coordinated action, provides a beginning means of assessing the fragility curves of organizations engaged in coordinated performance. It also offers a plausible explanation for differences in response to sudden threat by different organizations operating in disaster environments. Other factors also affect the ability of organizations to adapt to changing environments, and identifying these factors contributes to the careful assessment of organizational capacity to function under stress. Analyzing rapidly evolving response systems following earthquakes, I identified four types of adaptation that may be applicable to interorganizational systems that emerge in response to other types of hazards, including terrorist attacks (Comfort 1999). Looking more carefully at some of the individual incidents reported following the 9-11 attacks, one can identify these four types of adaptation in the record of transactions reported in public documents and newspapers. There may be others, but this characterization gives a gross classification of the types of interorganizational response systems that emerged under differing technical, organizational, and cultural conditions in environments of shared risk.

TYPES OF ADAPTATION IN RESPONSE TO THREAT

In their classic book, *Order Out of Chaos*, Ilya Prigogine and Isabelle Stengers (1984) identified the sensitive dependence of emergent systems upon the set of initial conditions that characterized their operating environment. In examining the emergence of rapidly evolving response systems following earthquakes, I found a set of basic characteristics that influenced the types of adaptation achieved in 11 field studies. These conditions are described more fully in my book, *Shared Risk: Complex Systems in Seismic Response* (999), but I mention them briefly here as conditions that affect the emergence of response systems under threat, including terrorist attacks. The four basic conditions include:

- Articulation of commonly understood meanings between a system and its members

- Sufficient trust among leaders, organizations, and citizens to enable members to accept direction

- Sufficient resonance between the emerging system and its environment to gain support for action

- Sufficient resources to sustain collective action under varying conditions

The most critical condition of the set for the emergence of coordinated action is the first. Without a common understanding of the threat, participants in an emerging system are unable to act. Trust is also critical to overcome uncertainty. Resonance, or support of the community, as well as the necessary resources, are essential for collective action. As the response systems begin to emerge, they are further affected by three different sets of characteristics. Each system can be characterized by technical, organizational, and cultural indicators. The technical indicators include measures of the technical structure, e.g. transportation, electrical power structure, communications. Organizational indicators include measures of organizational flexibility, e.g. adaptability to changing conditions, style of communication among members, leadership or lack thereof. Cultural indicators include cultural openness, e.g. willingness to accept new concepts, new patterns of action. The emerging systems vary in terms of the indicators, and the interaction among these three sets limits the system's capacity for adaptation to a damaged environment. The response systems reflect these limits, defined largely by the initial conditions in which the damaging event occurred. The four types of adaptive systems identified in field studies of earthquake response systems, briefly, are: nonadaptive systems, emergent adaptive systems, operative adaptive systems, and auto-adaptive systems.

Nonadaptive systems are systems that are low on technical structure, low on organizational flexibility, and low on cultural openness to new information. They function under threat largely dependent upon outside assistance, but revert to previous status after the threatening event. Emergent adaptive systems are low on technical structure, medium on organizational flexibility, and medium on cultural openness to new concepts of operation and organization. These systems develop a mode of organization and action to cope with the threat during disaster operations, but are unable to sustain collective action after the immediate threat passes. Operative adaptive systems are those that are medium on technical structure, medium on organizational flexibility, and medium on cultural openness to new information. These systems function well in response to threat, but prove unable to translate methods of response into new modes of sustained operation and threat reduction. Auto-adaptive systems are those systems that are high on technical structure, high on organizational flexibility, and high on cultural openness to new information. Such systems represent a rare achievement, but in practice, these systems prove effective in response to threat and are able to transfer lessons learned from prior experience into a sustained reduction of threat.

In terms of organizational fragility observed in the events of 9-11, the organizational subsystems that represented the flights from Boston into the World Trade Center illustrate nonadaptive systems. Both flights showed the collapse of sensemaking, as crews and passengers confronted previously unthinkable events. Cut off from communications with their air traffic control towers, the crews had no access to external assistance. Following previous procedures that likely anticipated negotiations with the hijackers, the passengers apparently waited for further instructions. Crews and passengers were unable to recognize the danger, and therefore unable to act.

Flight #93 from Newark illustrates an emergent adaptive system. Given similar circumstances as the flights from Boston, the hijackers moved to take control of the plane. But the passengers, through the use of cell phones, learned of the crashes into the World Trade Center. With this information, they were able to recognize the threat and mobilized as an emergent system to thwart the hijackers. The plane crashed in the struggle, and all lives were lost in the process, but the self organization of the crew and passengers to take collective action stands as striking evidence of organizational capacity for adaptation in response to threat.

The response of the federal agencies to the attacks illustrates an operative adaptive system. With judgment honed in response to severe natural disasters, senior personnel at the Federal Emergency Management Agency, the U.S. Army Corps of Engineers, the Department of Health and Human Services, and the National Communications Services collaborated in rapid mobilization of response to both the World Trade Center and Pentagon sites simultaneously. Informed by previous experience in training exercises and actual disaster operations, these personnel were familiar with the resources available for response and the capacities of each agency, and were able to communicate easily across agency and jurisdictional lines. Resources were committed upon verbal request, with paperwork to follow, in order to expedite the mobilization of the response system, illustrating the trust and professional respect shared among the operating agencies. But it remains to be seen whether the federal agencies are able to integrate their performance with state, county, and local agencies successfully in a broader, more unified effort to reduce the risk of terrorism before damaging events occur. The ease with which the hijackers had operated in the U.S. society, entering the country despite previous suspicious acts and leaving a disparate trail of evidence that showed repeated contacts among their network, reveals gaps in the integration of information from different sources that might have identified and interrupted the terrorist acts before they occurred. Developing the fourth type, an auto-adaptive system, is the most critical in a continued effort to anticipate and reduce the threat of terrorism or other hazards. It means integrating the emergency response agencies at local, county, state, and federal jurisdictional levels into a unified system that can easily share information and resources among agencies at each jurisdictional level, and across jurisdictional levels. In the case of international terrorism, as represented by the events of September 11, it means extending this network of communication and coordination to work with other emergency response agencies around the globe.

NEXT STEPS

The threat of terrorism continues. If it is not the al Qaeda network, it is radical groups that threaten abortion clinics and public figures, or troubled teen-agers who bring guns to schools. It is clearly a "man-made hazard," stemming from the discontents, inequalities, and unsolved problems of our society and the global community, but it is not likely to disappear easily or quickly. Governmental agencies that have legal responsibility for emergency response will need new methods of identifying and disabling such threats to protect public security.

The important lesson from September 11 is optimistic. Governmental agencies can and do learn, and public personnel adapt their behavior to meet increasing demands. But facilitating the rate and mode of learning within and between agencies is a major task in a society as large, complex, and diverse as the United States. In a culture that prizes individualism and independent action, the uncertainty created by terrorist threats requires a different form of action, one in which individuals can function effectively in interdependent systems to achieve a collective goal of public security.

Based on a brief review of emergency response actions following the September 11 events, I offer three recommendations for strategies to increase governmental performance in risk reduction and response to hazardous events. First, we may improve interorganizational performance in the complex environment of disaster by studying systematically the conditions under which organizations fail, and identifying the break-points in the systems and sub-systems that are vulnerable to different kinds of stresses. By learning more about how and when organizations fail, we will also learn new methods of reinforcing them, and devise more effective patterns of communication and coordination to make them more resilient under increasing demands and urgent time pressure. Devising and testing measures of fragility and resilience in organizational systems will contribute significantly to our ability to maintain self-organizing, auto-adaptive emergency response systems.

Second, we must recognize that emergency operations are, by definition, nonlinear and dynamic, and that rational, linear models of problem solving and management will almost certainly fail under the urgent stress of disaster. Instead of a step-wise emergency plan where each lower jurisdiction operates alone until it exhausts its resources before requesting assistance from the next jurisdiction, it is constructive to acknowledge emergency response as an interjurisdictional problem that escalates and de-escalates over varying conditions and time. Combining the concept of fragility curves for an interorganizational system with the recognition of shared responsibility among the actors in this system, it is possible to create a more appropriate sharing of tasks that would maximize the skills, knowledge, and resources of the different jurisdictions in a smoothly operating, more efficient response system. As different points on the fragility curve of the interorganizational response system are breached, those conditions would trigger response from the appropriate organizations and jurisdictions participating in the response system.

For example, if a fire broke out in a residential backyard, it would elicit a response from the local fire department, and the municipality would provide 100 percent of the resources and effort to suppress the fire. But if the fire approached a storage site with hazardous materials, the increased risk may lead to a request for the county hazardous materials team, and the municipality and county would share the effort in response operations at 60 percent municipality and 40 percent county. If the hazardous materials at the storage site required greater expertise in containing the threat than the county team possessed, state assistance might be needed, and the shared responsibility might shift to 40 percent municipal, 30 percent county, and 30 percent state. If the evidence at the site indicated a deliberate intent to explode hazardous materials to threaten the community, the balance of responsibility might shift again to 15 percent municipal, 20 percent county, 25 percent state, and 40 percent federal. Each jurisdictional level would contribute knowledge, skills, and expertise at the level most appropriate to bring the threat under control most quickly and efficiently. The jurisdictional responsibilities indeed overlap, but the calculation of responsibility and allocation of resources and skills are based first on the identified requirements of the situation and second on the accounting procedures of the respective jurisdictions.

Third, maintaining public security in the face of uncertain threat and hazards will require a substantial investment in information technology to facilitate the continuous process of organizational learning essential to achieve an auto-adaptive, self-organizing emergency response system. Auto-adaptive systems depend upon the development of an information infrastructure that can support the rapid transitions from normal to extreme operations in sudden emergencies. Such systems enable communities to withstand extreme events and to translate that experience into informed actions for future protection. With thoughtful reflection, this may be the enduring legacy of September 11.

ACKNOWLEDGEMENTS

I express my appreciation to the Alan K. Campbell Institute at Syracuse University for inviting me to participate in this symposium. I acknowledge with thanks and appreciation John R. Harrald and Joseph L. Barbera, co-principal investigators of National Science Foundation grant #CM530309, "Observing and Documenting the Inter-organizational Response to the September 11 Attacks," for including me on their research team. I thank Michael Carrigan and Naim Kapucu, graduate students at the University of Pittsburgh, who assisted me with the content analysis of the *New York Times*.

REFERENCES

Alberts, D.S., J.J. Garstka, and F.P. Stein, 1999. *Network Centric Warfare: Developing and Leveraging Information Superiority* (2nd Ed. Rev.). Washington, D.C.: DOD Command and Control Research Program.

Argyris and Schon. 1996. *Organizational Learning II: Theory, Method and Practice*. Reading, MA: Addison-Wesley.

Axelrod, Robert. 1997. *The Complexity of Cooperation: Agent-based Models of Competition and Collaboration*. Princeton, N.J.: Princeton University Press.

Casciati, F. and L. Faravelli. 1991. *Fragility Analysis of Complex Structural Systems*. Taunton, Somerset, England: Research Studies Press; New York: J. Wiley.

Chopra, A.K. and R. K. Goel. 1999. "Capacity-Design-Diagram Methods Based on Inelastic Design Spectrum." In *Earthquake Spectra*, Vol. 15, No. 4 (November): 637-656.

Comfort, Louise K. 1999. *Shared Risk: Complex Systems in Seismic Response*. Oxford: Pergamon Press.

Dror, Yehezkel. 1987. *Policy Making under Adversity*. New Brunswick, NJ: Transaction Books.

Federal Emergency Management Agency. 1999. *Federal Emergency Response Plan*. Washington, D.C.: Federal Emergency Management Agency.

Flin, Rhona. 1996. *Sitting in the Hot Seat: Leaders and Teams for Critical Incident Management*. Chicester: John Wiley and Sons.

Fritsch, Jane. "As Others Flee, Scores of Firefighters Dash Into Towers to Help; Many Do Not Return." *New York Times*. 12 Sept. 2001. p. A2.

Kauffman, Stuart A. 1993. *The Origins of Order: Self-Organization and Selection in Evolution*. New York: Oxford University Press.

Klein, Gary A. 1993. "A Recognition Primed Decision Making (RPD) Model of Rapid Decision Making." In G. Klein, J. Orasanu, R. Calderwood, and C. Zsambok, eds. *Decision Making in Action: Models and Methods*. Norwood, NJ: Ablex Publishing Corporation. pp. 138-147.

McKelvey, B. 2001. "MicroStrategy from MacroLeadership: Distributed Intelligence via New Science." In A.Y. Lewin and H. Volberda, eds. *Mobilizing the Self-Renewing Organization*. Thousand Oaks, CA: Sage.

New York Times, September 12 – October 6, 2001.

Perez-Pena, Richard. "Trying to Command and Emergency When the Emergency Command Center Is Gone." *New York Times*. 12 Sept. 2001. p. A7.

Prigogine, Ilya and Isabelle Stengers. 1984. *Order Out of Chaos: Man's New Dialogue with Nature*. New York: Bantam Books, Inc.

Simon, Herbert A. 1981. *The Sciences of the Artificial*, 2nd Ed. Cambridge, MA: MIT Press.

Weick, Karl E. 1995. *Sensemaking in Organizations*. Thousand Oaks, CA: Sage Publications.

Weick, Karl E. 2001. *Making Sense of the Organization*. Oxford, Malden, MA: Blackwell Business, 2001.

PUBLIC SERVICE REFORM AND THE NEW SECURITY AGENDA

Donald P. Moynihan
Alasdair Roberts

Never before September 11 had Americans experienced so devastating an attack on their own land. Its financial and military centers hit, with thousands of casualties; the president removed to a secure airbase; the transcontinental air transport system frozen; and fighters patrolling the skies. In the weeks that followed, new horror: death delivered by anthrax-contaminated letters, and fear of worse contagions. Then a full-scale war, in which American and allied troops toppled a regime almost exactly half a world away. Still more: aborted hijackings, a crackdown on individuals and organizations thought to sympathize with terrorists, and talk of war against other "rogue states."

Throughout these months, Americans looked to government for assurance that public safety would be protected. "Homeland security" was a phrase unknown to most Americans before September 11 — in fact, a phrase that would have seemed alien to the American vocabulary. After September 11, it became the touchstone for policymakers in every part of government. A new Office of Homeland Security calculated that it would be required to coordinate the work of over 40 federal agencies. The war on terrorism has blurred distinctions between foreign and domestic policy, or military and civilian affairs.

The events of Fall 2001 have shaped the United States in many ways — its sense of security, its cultural preoccupations, its foreign relations and military policy. The crisis also tested the capabilities of our public institutions. Public agencies responsible for a broad range of functions — intelligence, law enforcement, emergency response, immigration and border control, public health, defense — bore heavy and urgent responsibilities. Some agencies surpassed expectations, and many public employees gave their lives to protect their fellow citizens. However, weeks of intensive media and legislative scrutiny showed that the performance of other public agencies had been lackluster, or dangerously inadequate.

There is a community of academics and policymakers who specialize in the subject of government reform, who have an obvious interest in examining the results from this test of governmental capabilities. They need to ask the following questions: How have the events of Fall 2001 and its aftermath reshaped perceptions about the role of government and the goals of public sector reform? Has the new focus on public security placed us at a critical juncture in the evolution of public management policy? There is evidence that some widely accepted public management prescriptions for reform are now under challenge. How broad and durable are these challenges likely to be? This paper offers a preliminary account of the how the public security agenda could reshape the wider public management policy agenda.

Historically, public service reform is not a subject that had a high public profile. This changed in the 1980s and 1990s. Governments in many established democracies began highly visible projects to refurnish their public sectors. The motives for reform were obvious. Since the early 1970s, these governments had accumulated large amounts of debt, and the habit of deficit spending could not be continued. Fiscal pressures drove governments to cut unneeded programs, or find creative ways of making government "work better and cost less." Compounding these fiscal pressures was a severe, long-term decline in respect for government. Major government initiatives of the 1960s and 1970s were now regarded as costly failures. "Market solutions" — rather than direct government interventions — became the preferred method for responding to policy problems.

In the United States — and elsewhere — government was on the defensive, attempting to reverse the corrosive effects of fiscal stress and eroding legitimacy. The Clinton administration's eight-year project to "reinvent government," led by the Vice President Gore's National Performance Review, represented one high-profile attempt to affirm the relevance of government. Other governments launched similar projects to "modernize" their public services. These reform efforts had common themes: lean administration, with reduction of non-essential spending and "top-heavy" management; more emphasis on results, and particularly on customer service; and more extensive reliance on contractors and "public-private partnerships." The Organization for Economic Cooperation and Development argued that governments had found a "new paradigm" for organizing public services, which soon became known as the "new public management," or NPM.[1] In the United States, NPM ideas were more commonly referred to as "reinventing government", or simply "reinvention."

Even before September 11, many observers — and some governments — had begun to question the merits of the reinvention paradigm. Fiscal pressures had begun to ease, and some costs of new policies had become apparent. Some commentators had even suggested the emergence of a "post-NPM" agenda, less vigorous in its pursuit of some elements of the reinvention paradigm. But the change should not be overestimated. In June 2001, the OECD sketched a familiar picture of the "government of the future": still laboring to reclaim the trust of citizens, demonstrate its capacity to deliver programs efficiently, and establish its place in a market society (Organization for Economic Cooperation and Development 2001).

The events of Fall 2001 have changed the context and priorities for reform. Faith in government has suddenly rebounded, and fiscal constraints have been loosened. Some of the dangers of a preoccupation with lean administration or client satisfaction have become more evident. Ambivalence about the private provision of key services has become more pronounced. The critical importance of interagency and intergovernmental collaboration has been emphasized. This is not a complete turnabout in reform priorities. Nevertheless, the new security agenda seems likely to be less hesitant about asserting a role for government, and on preferring direct public provision; more careful about balancing client satisfaction with enforcement functions; and attentive to the challenges of coordination.

SHIFTS IN CONTEXT

Government Matters

Perhaps the most striking change since September 11 has been the sudden shift in views about the significance of government. The shift in

attitudes is notable not just in itself, but because it may signal an acceptance, and expectation, that the federal government will become more
active, spend more money, and widen the scope of its functions. For two
decades, government's role has been diminished; often, it has been the
object of ridicule. At best, government was said to be irrelevant, rendered impotent by globalization and technological change. At worst, it
was incompetent, stifling growth with heavy-handed regulation and taxa-
tion. The era of big government is over, President Bill Clinton told us in
1996 — an accurate reflection of the prevailing sentiment, even if social
and regulatory programs remained extensive by historical standards.

September 11 changed this view of the public sector. The attacks
reminded us that there are basic functions of state — the protection of
personal safety, the maintenance of social and economic order — that
remain profoundly important. It was noteworthy that President Bush —
a conservative elected on a promise of restraint — promised, within
minutes of the attacks, to respond with "the full resources of the federal
government." The Bush administration became an "energetic executive,"
to use Hamilton's phrase. (Perhaps too energetic, in the eyes of some
civil libertarians.) The hesitation that had distinguished the earlier phase
of government reform evaporated overnight. There was no long
deliberation, as there had been in preceding years, about whether there
was a public interest in direct government action.

The new view of government was reflected in the startling change in
public opinion about their trust in public institutions. Trust in government had been on a downward slide in the United States and other
established democracies for years, provoking alarm among many
academic commentators and policymakers. Most major reinvention programs had been motivated as instruments for reversing this decline of
confidence. In the United States, the Clinton Administration's National
Performance Review promised to "restore trust and strengthen
Americans' confidence that government can make a difference in their
lives" (National Partnership for Reinventing Government 2000).
(Similarly, Britain's Labour government aimed for a "restoration of faith"
in public institutions (Blair 1998).) The attacks quickly produced an
effect that reformers would have thought not practically unattainable a
few months before. According to a Washington Post poll completed in
October 2001, 64 percent of Americans trusted government to do what
is right most or all of the time — a level of support not seen in comparable
polls since the mid 1960s, and a dramatic contrast to the 20 percent
levels of trust found in the mid 1990s (Milbank and Morin 2001)(Table 1).

Table 1: How much of the time do you think you can trust government in Washington to do what is right?

	Just about always	Most of the time	Some of the time	Never
1966	17%	48%	28%	3%
1994	2%	18%	75%	5%
2000	4%	26%	64%	2%
2001	13%	51%	35%	1%

The new view of government was reflected more deeply in popular culture. In the days after September 11, the media emphasized stories about defiance in the face of fear, and found government workers who were indisputably heroic: firefighters, police officers, and other rescue workers who had risked their lives to save others. The image of fire trucks and rescue vehicles caught by the rubble of the collapsed World Trade Center towers, metaphors for the rescue workers who had died in the collapse, were affixed in collective memory. In the weeks to come, the dangers confronted by the armed forces and the mail service would also encourage deeper sympathy for government. The selfless actions and risks endured by public employees diluted much of the public cynicism that has grown around government in recent years. At Christmas, toy companies produced new action figures wearing the uniform of the New York Fire Department. *Time* magazine named Mayor Rudy Giuliani its man of the year.

Public opinion is volatile, and the levels of support attained in Fall 2001 may not be maintained. Nevertheless, high levels of support have already enabled the federal government to take steps that significantly extended the reach of government. Anti-terrorism legislation (the USA PATRIOT Act, adopted in late October) extended the investigative and arrest powers of federal law enforcement agencies. (Britain and Canada adopted similar laws.) Congress quickly established two new federal bodies — the Office of Homeland Security and the Transportation Security Administration — and endorsed more aggressive action by many other federal agencies. By the end of the 2001, support for the Bush administration remained high, and support for Congress had hit record levels. A large majority of Americans had confidence in the government's ability to protect them from future attacks (*Washington Post* 2001).

Loosening Fiscal Constraints

An immediate consequence of the new war of terrorism was a diminution in concern about control of taxing and spending. Persistent deficits in the quarter-century after 1973 led many governments to prioritize fiscal control — what British and Canadian policymakers liked to call "prudence" — in budgeting. Much energy was invested in the task of inventing tools for promoting fiscal control: balanced budget laws, lockboxes, ad hoc program reviews, and tighter procedures for reviewing proposed new expenditures. Budgetary balance became the new "golden rule." By 1998, the drive for fiscal control had largely succeeded: many governments began achieving budgetary balance for the first time in three decades (Patshnik 1999).

An economic slowdown had already begun testing the commitment to prudence before September 11. But the attacks on Washington and New York seemed to change the rules overnight. Within days, Congress appropriated $40 billion in emergency spending, soon followed by a $15 billion rescue for airline companies. It was not deterred by forecasts that federal deficits would reemerge in 2002. In January 2002, Congress appropriated another $20 billion for homeland security, and in addition approved the biggest increase in defense appropriations in over a decade. Britain's Chancellor of the Exchequer and Canada's Minister of Finance also announced increased spending on defense and domestic security — and their first projected budget deficits in three years.

NEW PRIORITIES IN MANAGEMENT REFORM

More positive perceptions in government were accompanied with higher expectations with regard to public security. The emphasis on public security set the stage for the creation and acceptance of new priorities in government reform. In some cases these new priorities directly challenged the organizational principles promoted by reinvention.

Preparing for the Immeasurable and Unpredictable

Reinvention seemed most powerful as a toolkit for dealing with what were sometimes called the "factory operations" of government — agencies that performed highly routinized work, such as the Patent and Trademark Office or the Social Security Administration. Of course, this work was socially important, and often involved the exercise of discretion by agency staff. Nonetheless, the number of transactions was large, and the character of those transactions predictable. Work processes could be easily broken down and reengineered. These agencies were easily subjected to performance-reporting requirements, because there were many things that could be measured, and measurements could be easily compared from one year to the next.

In some respects, the crisis did test some of these "factory operations," such as the Bureau of Consular Affairs, responsible for processing millions of non-immigrant visas a year, or the Immigration and Naturalization Service, which conducts roughly half-a-billion inspections of individuals entering over 300 ports of entry every year. And the crisis did reveal some costs of a decade-long emphasis on "lean production" within such agencies. Doris Meissner, former head of the INS, complained that the American consulates had been put on a "starvation diet" for most of the decade, undermining the capacity to do effective screening. In one Middle Eastern consulate, entry-level officers were reported to process almost five hundred visa applications a day. At home, a few hundred Border Patrol employees had been left to watch the vast 7,500-mile border between the United States and Canada.

Routine functions are important; but the crisis also reminds us of the importance of the immeasurable and unpredictable. Many government operations tested in the last few months are not easily disassembled and monitored. Law enforcement activities or military operations may follow twisting paths, strewn with unexpected obstacles and lucky breaks. Objectives may shift in mid-stream as new intelligence is gathered. Sometimes it may be impossible, for reasons of diplomacy or national security, to report candidly on the effectiveness of some operations. Key outcomes (security, for example) are difficult to describe concretely or measure easily, and the connection between action and outcome is horrendously complex.

And we must prepare for the unpredictable. Our preoccupation with routine operations may have dulled our attention to the importance of planning for rare but catastrophic events. In quieter times, the capacity to handle the unpredictable — that is, organizational readiness — may look to some observers like wastefulness, or proof of organizational inertia. (*Why do we have underemployed staff? Why are we stockpiling smallpox vaccine, years after its eradication?*) But crisis quickly reveals problems in readiness. Throughout September and October, health care providers reported their ability to handle spikes in demand for services had worn away. The *New York Times* reported:

For more than a decade, managed care companies and the Medicare system have pressed hospitals to squeeze the extras out of their budgets. Hospitals have cut beds from emergency rooms. They have eliminated laboratory technician positions and pharmacy jobs. They no longer stockpile medicines, and instead buy drugs each day as needed. These steps have eliminated what is known as surge capacity, the ability to handle a sharp increase in patients. (Stolberg)

Law enforcement agencies dealt with their own weaknesses in "surge capacity," as they struggled to balance new responsibilities and existing caseloads. And our failure to plan for the unanticipated became evident in other ways. Throughout the fall, the nation's only laboratory with capacity to make anthrax vaccine remained out of service: it had been partly dismantled in early October for cleaning. Readiness is critical to public sector performance; but gauging how much readiness we have — or ought to have — may be a neglected challenge.

Rethinking Privatization

The crisis may encourage closer scrutiny of another important theme in the reinvention program: privatization. Much of scrutiny was directed to weaknesses in the screening of airline passengers, which since 1973 has been conducted by contractors hired by airlines. It is a highly competitive industry, driven by intense pressure from airlines to lower costs. The security industry employs a poorly educated workforce that is rarely paid more than the minimum wage. Morale is abysmal, and annual employee turnover in some firms exceeds 90 percent. The industry also proved difficult to regulate. Attempts by the Federal Aviation Administration and airport administrators to improve contractor performance often proved ineffective (Moss and Eaton 2001). Some critics said that contracting-out also discouraged data sharing with law enforcement agencies.

More to the point, the industry appeared unable to assure security. Even after September 11, there were frequent reports of security breaches at major airports. In mid-November, the president signed the Aviation Security Act, which turned airport security functions into a direct federal responsibility. The new Transportation Security Administration was given one year to recruit 28,000 employees — a task that had already proved daunting by early 2002. In a federal civilian workforce of 2.6 million, the significance of this step should not be overstated. Nevertheless, the decision had symbolic importance: Congress had determined that a prerequisite for the restoration of public confidence was placing security work in the hands of public employees.

There were other areas where privatization garnered closer attention. The nation's only anthrax vaccine producer was, as it happened, a privately owned company: BioPort of Lansing, Michigan. Like airport security firms, BioPort had also been criticized for deficiencies in performance. The Department of Defense, a major client, stopped using BioPort's vaccine in 1997, and in Fall 2001 the firm was undergoing a review by the Food and Drug Administration. It had failed FDA reviews in each of the preceding three years. In November 2001, the Gilmore Commission on terrorism concluded that "direct government ownership or sponsorship is likely to be the only reasonable answer" for anthrax vaccine production (Gilmore Commission 2001: 8).

September 11 also affected the privatization agenda in other contexts. In July, the British government sold its air traffic control agency, NATS, to a consortium of British airlines. The viability of the privatization was threatened by the sharp decline in trans-oceanic traffic following the September 11 attacks. The government made plans to rescue the project with a cash bailout that would restore its majority ownership in the agency. In its February 2001 budget, the Bush administration had suggested that the British reform (and a comparable Canadian effort) could be a model for privatization of U.S. air traffic control functions — but the probability of this is now sharply dimmed.

The decision to federalize airline security and closer scrutiny of other privatization proposals represents a remarkable about-turn in public management policy, at least with respect to the provision of services relevant to public security. NPM ideas had reinforced well-established ideological presumptions that markets were superior to government bureaucracies, and that governments should be constantly pared of any function that could be provided by the private sector. In the United States, privatization of services was institutionalized and vigorously pursued as an administrative procedure through OMB Circular A-76. (Other countries adopted similar schemes, such as Britain's compulsory competitive tendering initiative.) Federalization of airline security marks an unusual reverse in the otherwise steady flow of services from the public to the private sector. The newly established prominence of public security concerns offers a justification for the public provision of certain services, making it more difficult to argue that the private sector is better equipped to deliver these services effectively. Where there is a potential for private provision of services to create security risks that may prove catastrophic in terms of loss of life and property, the public sector will be increasingly involved.

Customer Service

Improving customer service was another main goal of the reinvention program. In fact, employee surveys suggested that the emphasis on responsiveness to customer needs was one of the main legacies of the Clinton administration's eight-year reform program (National Partnership for Reinventing Government, 1998). The administration encouraged federal agencies with a "high impact" on the public to develop service standards and regularly collect data on customer satisfaction. According to a recent study by the University of Michigan Business School, client satisfaction with services provided by many major agencies has improved significantly (University of Michigan Business School 2001).

At the same time, the rhetoric of customer service often aggravated many observers, who argued that many agencies had regulatory or enforcement functions that could be undermined by a preoccupation with client satisfaction. Before September 11, the Internal Revenue Service was considered by critics to be a good example of the pitfalls of such a preoccupation. The IRS suffered a public pummeling in 1998 as Senate hearings highlighted stories of overzealous agents abusing their enforcement powers. Designated as a "high-impact agency," the IRS took steps to restore public confidence. But critics argued that this involved an excessive reduction in enforcement activities. A recent study has showed that audit rates declined by almost 70 percent between 1995 and 2000 (Johnston 2001). Another of the Clinton administration's "high-impact agencies" — the Food and Drug Administration — has been subject to similar criticism (Washburn 2001).

Several agencies now at the forefront of the war on terrorism were also tagged as "high-impact agencies" and told to emphasize improved customer service. The crisis has encouraged a new balancing of priorities. Before September 11, the INS and Customs Service shared a major performance goal in the area of border facilitation; to attain land border wait times of less than 20 minutes 80 percent of the time, and clear over 70 percent of commercial air flights through primary inspection in 30 minutes or less. These targets became infeasible after September 11. An innovation intended to ease land border crossings — dedicated commuter lanes — was suspended. The Bureau of Consular Affairs had pledged, as one of its "high-impact" goals, to make permanent its Visa Waiver Pilot Program. The attacks brought renewed attention to earlier complaints by the Justice Department's Inspector General that "the greatest risk to national security and illegal immigration" arose from nonimmigrants visiting under the program (Norman 2001).

Regulatory Partnerships

Another group of governmental clients — regulated industries — also found that federal agencies were taking a new, tougher view of their responsibilities. The reinvention paradigm emphasized "regulatory partnerships," in which agencies would "negotiate, not dictate" to achieve its goals (National Performance Review 1995: 4). After September 11, agencies in key sectors began to adopt firmer positions. The Nuclear Regulatory Commission announced a "top-to-bottom review" of its rules on security at the country's 100 nuclear plants, notwithstanding industry assurances about the adequacy of current policy (Grunwald and Behr 2001).

Relations with the influential pharmaceutical industry also became more difficult. Shortly after the anthrax attacks of early October, pressure grew in Washington for the government to invoke statutory rules that would allow widespread production of ciprofloxacin, an anthrax antibiotic whose patent, held by the German drug company Bayer AG, did not expire until 2003. Bayer quickly consented to an agreement with Health and Human Services Secretary Tommy Thompson under which it would provide a 100-million-pill stockpile of the drug at one-third of its market price. The Canadian government went further, quickly authorizing the production of ciprofloxacin by a rival manufacturer.

These actions had larger costs for the pharmaceutical industry. The administration's action made it difficult to resist calls at the World Trade Organization negotiations in Doha, Qatar, for an agreement acknowledging the right of developing countries to breach drug patents to combat public health crises such as AIDS. At home, the industry worried that the cipro controversy might provoke a larger debate about rising drug prices. *Business Week* called the pressure on Bayer AG remarkable — especially for a "free-market Republican administration" (Carey and Barrett 2001).

CHALLENGES OF COORDINATION

As the federal government deals with public security and terrorism issues, it faces the fact that traditional governmental structures, built around the regulation and direct delivery of services within a nation state, are no longer adequate. Improved coordination appears necessary if different federal agencies, levels of domestic government, and nation states are to pursue closely aligned goals in some sort of collective fashion. Just how such collaboration can be structured to work effectively remains unclear.

Interagency and Intergovernmental Coordination

Much of the reinvention agenda emphasized problems that government encountered at the front-line of service delivery. Its key aim was the production of better services, at lower cost. The higher-level functions of government — coordination among agencies, formulation of policy, long-range planning — were not among its major concerns. On the contrary, the higher levels of government were often disparaged as organizational deadweight, whose meddling impaired the flexibility and efficiency of lower-level operations.

Even before September 11, governments had recognized the limits of this approach to reform. They worried that the preoccupation with service production might have aggravated the problem of "stovepiping" within government, and looked for measures to overcome the insularity of agencies. "Horizontality" (the Canadian phrase) and "joined-upness" (the awkward British equivalent) were the new keywords.

The crisis has brought new attention to problems of coordination within the U.S. government. The September 11 attacks highlighted failures in coordination within the intelligence community, between intelligence agencies and federal law enforcement agencies, and between the four agencies — INS, Customs Service, Coast Guard, and Bureau of Consular Affairs — responsible for border management. As the government anticipated future attacks, the number of federal agencies with a role in the anti-terrorism effort multiplied — a point neatly illustrated in a flowchart of federal responsibilities distributed by the White House in early November (Figure 1; (Mitchell 2001)).[2] The debate over the role of the new Office of Homeland Security — its operational role, if any; its budgetary authority; its place within the Executive Office of the President — revived a number of classical questions of coordination and control. The problem was technical, as well as organizational: agencies found that collaboration was sometimes confounded by poorly integrated or incompatible information systems.

This is only one part of the coordination problem — the challenge of *intragovernmental* collaboration. At the same time there were complex problems of *intergovernmental* collaboration. While federal, state, and local authorities seemed to coordinate their response to attacks in New York effectively, the situation seemed less satisfactory in Washington.

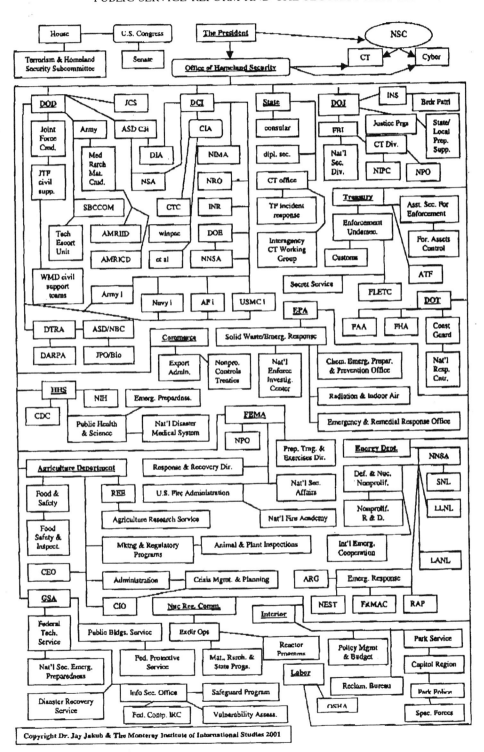

Copyright Dr. Jay Jakub & The Monterey Institute of International Studies 2001

Emergency personnel from neighboring jurisdictions found they simply could not communicate with one another, while Mayor Anthony Williams complained about the federal government's slowness in providing information about unfolding events. Williams later called intergovernmental cooperation the "biggest challenge" in the war against terrorism (Lehrer 2001).

Problems of *transnational* collaboration emerged as well. Prevailing public management theory offers little guidance, as the reinvention agenda was primarily about the reshaping of federal, state and local functions, not about dealing with transnational public problems. The negotiations between U.S. and Canadian agencies about coordination of law enforcement and border control activities, and the reconciliation of their contrasting immigration and asylum policies, is an obvious example of the practical relationships between transnational collaboration and public security. The two governments negotiated an accord in December 2001 intended to ensure that the new emphasis on security did not cripple economic relations between the United States and its largest trading partner. Larger problems of transnational collaboration arose as law enforcement and intelligence agencies intensified their work with overseas counterparts in tracking down the al Qaeda network, and as allies planned military action in Afghanistan. The unilateralism that was thought to characterize the early months of the Bush administration became a thing of the past.

THE NEW SECURITY AGENDA

Admittedly, it is important not to exaggerate the impact of the crisis on the reinvention paradigm. There may be sectors of government that are largely unaffected by recent events, where the influence of the New Public Management remains unimpaired. The crisis itself may also ebb. The sense of imminent danger could be eased by military accomplishment. Investigations could highlight failures in planning and response, and new extensions of governmental authority could prove less effective than hoped. (In fact, there is an underlying irony in the recent surge in respect for government: the problem that has triggered this surge is also one of the most intractable problems that could be posed to government.) On the other hand, the pendulum is unlikely to swing back quickly. Institutional changes made in the last three months will be carried on by inertia, if nothing else. And the perception of risk is likely to remain large enough to encourage caution about aggressive application of NPM principles in areas that seem relevant to public security.

The New Public Management — or reinvention — will not be wholly overturned, but it may be sufficiently qualified that it will no longer be useful to talk about it in the same way as before. Reinvention was presented as a paradigmatic shift in public management: a wholly distinct way of thinking about the structure of public services. The events of the last four months have revealed the malleable, contingent character of this paradigm. The sudden prominence of public security as a policy priority caused a quick and unhesitating abandonment of ideas that were integral to the reinvention paradigm. Basic tenets of the reinvention paradigm – privatization, customer service, regulatory partnerships – were put aside in the face of a threat to public safety; while other tenets, such as improved performance in routine and measurable functions, were deemed less important than building capacity to deal with the unexpected.

However, the steps taken to bolster public security cannot be said to signal another paradigmatic change in public management theory. It is clearly limited in scope to certain functions and unconcerned with the bulk of the public sector. What emerges, therefore, is an evolution in public management theory. The reinvention paradigm will continue to be influential, but with careful consideration of public security issues in relevant services. This altered reform agenda will be more careful about planning for contingencies in the fields of public health and security, more cautious about customer service in some sectors, more cautious about active programs of privatization, and more attentive to problems of coordination and collaboration. On the whole, this suggests a more conservative reform agenda, aimed at buttressing the capacity of existing public institutions. This will reinforce new themes already emerging before September 11, such as concern about the looming "human capital crisis" within public services and worry about the erosion of physical infrastructure.

Ultimately, terrorism recalls the need for a state that is whole rather than atomized, comforting rather than threatening. Terrorists struck with a combination of great determination and some ingenuity. As government tries to patch the vulnerabilities central to an open and free society, we know, in truth, that the job will never be fully complete, and as a consequence, we will never fully be safe. While the state will likely be criticized for specific failures to anticipate or deal with terrorist events, our overall need to believe in a protective actor is likely to prevail over such criticisms. In times such as this, citizens will look for an institutional focal point upon which to concentrate the hopes and confidence of protection. The market does not provide a suitable candidate, nor does supranational institutions. As before, in times of crisis, the traditional nation state is dusted down and reestablished as the center of our attention. The question is, is government up to the task?

REFERENCES

Blair, Tony (1998). *The Third Way: New Politics for a New Century*. London: Fabian Society. September 21, 1998.

Carey, John and Amy Barrett (2001). "Drug Prices: What's Fair?" *Business Week* 3761 (December 10, 2001): 60.

Gilmore Commission (2001). *Advance Executive Summary of Third Annual Report*. Washington, D.C.: RAND. November 1, 2001. (Advisory Panel to Assess Domestic Response Capabilities for Terrorism Involving Weapons of Mass Destruction).

Grunwald, Michael and Peter Behr (2001). "Are the Nation's Nuclear Power Plants Secure?" *Washington Post*. Washington, D.C. November 4, 2001. A16.

Hood, Christopher (1991). "A Public Management for all Seasons?" *Public Administration* 69.1: 3-20.

Johnston, David Cay (2001). "A Smaller IRS Gives up Billions in Back Taxes." *New York Times*. April 13, 2001. A1.

Lehrer, Jim (2001). The Newshour with Jim Lehrer. Washington, D.C.: MacNeil/Lehrer Productions. November 1, 2001.

Milbank, Dana and Richard Morin (2001). "Public is Unyielding in War against Terror." *Washington Post*. Washington, D.C. September 29, 2001. A1.

Mitchell, Alison (2001). "Disputes Erupt on Ridge's Needs for His Job." *New York Times*. New York. November 4, 2001. B7.

Moss, Michael and Leslie Eaton (2001). "Security Firms Ever Mindful to Cut Costs." *New York Times*. November 15, 2001. B1.

National Partnership for Reinventing Government (2000). *Creating a Culture of Change and Reconnecting Americans to their Government*. Washington, DC: National Partnership for Reinventing Government. April 2000.

National Performance Review (1995). *Common Sense Government: Works Better and Costs Less*. Washington, D.C.: National Performance Review. August 1995.

Norman, Bob (2001). "Admitting Terror." *Miami New Times*. Miami, FL. October 18, 2001.

Organization for Economic Cooperation and Development (2001). *Government of the Future*. Paris: OECD. June 2001. PUMA Policy Brief No. 9.

Stolberg, Sheryl Gay (2001). "Struggling to Reach a Consensus on Preparations for Bioterrorism." *New York Times*. New York. November 5, 2001. B1.

University of Michigan Business School (2001). *The American Customer Satisfaction Index: Special Report on Government Satisfaction Scores*. Ann Arbor, MI: University of Michigan Business School. December 17, 2001.

Washburn, Jennifer (2001). "Undue Influence." *The American Prospect* 12.14. August 13, 2001.

Washington Post (2001). Washington Post-ABC news poll: America at war. *Washington Post*. Washington, DC. November 28, 2001.

ENDNOTES

1 The phrase was coined by Christopher Hood of the London School of Economics (Hood 1991).

2 This chart was prepared by Dr. Jay Jakub, Staff Director of the House Subcommittee on Terrorism and Homeland Security. It is reproduced with his permission.

NOTE ON
CONTRIBUTORS

Michael Barkun (Ph.D., Northwestern University) is professor of political science in the Maxwell School. Among his books are *Religion and the Racist Right* (1997), which received the Myers Center Award; *Millennialism and Violence* (1996); and *Disaster and the Millennium* (1974). He is currently completing a book on the spread of conspiracy beliefs in America. He has been a consultant to the Critical Incident Response Group of the FBI. Prof. Barkun edits the *Religion and Politics* series, published by the Syracuse University Press, and serves on editorial boards of *Terror and Political Violence* and *Communal Studies*. He has been a recipient of grants from the Harry Frank Guggenheim Foundation, the Ford Foundation, and NEH.

Louise K. Comfort is a professor of public and international affairs at the University of Pittsburgh. She holds degrees in political science from Macalester College (B.A.); University of California, Berkeley (M.A.); and Yale University (Ph.D.). Her primary areas of research and teaching are in public policy analysis, decision making under conditions of uncertainty, and the mobilization of rapidly evolving systems in response to extreme events. Her most recent book is *Shared Risk: Complex Systems in Seismic Response* (Oxford and New York: Pergamon Press, 1999.) She is the principal investigator for the Interactive, Intelligent, Spatial Information System (IISIS) Project, housed at the University Center for Social and Urban Research, University of Pittsburgh. She is also an investigator on a National Science Foundation grant to study interorganizational coordination in response to the September 11 terror attacks.

Stephen Flynn is a senior fellow with the National Security Studies Program at the Council on Foreign Relations, where he is directing a national study group on "Protecting the Homeland: Rethinking the Role of Border Controls." He is also a commander in the U.S. Coast Guard, an associate professor of international relations, and a member of the permanent commissioned teaching staff at the U.S. Coast Guard Academy in New London, Connecticut. He served in the White House Military Office during the Bush administration, as a director for global issues on the National Security Council staff during the Clinton administration, and as a consultant on the homeland security issue to the U.S. Commission on National Security (Hart-Rudman Commission). He is author of several book chapters and articles on homeland security, border control, transportation security, and the illicit drug trade.

William Gormley is professor of government and public policy and associate dean of the Public Policy Institute at Georgetown University. Gormley is the author of several books on the bureaucracy and public policy, including most recently, *Organizational Report Cards*, with David Weimer. He is a fellow of the National Academy of Public Administration and president-elect of the American Political Science Association's Public Policy Section.

Stan Hawthorne is the partner-in-charge of PriceWaterhouseCoopers's services to the justice, law enforcement, and intelligence communities. A certified public accountant, he has led engagements involving large, complex reengineering and restructuring initiatives around enterprise-wide information systems assessments, planning, implementation, and strategy. He has provided testimony to Congress on numerous occasions. His clients include the U.S. Immigration and Naturalization Service, the Executive Office for U.S. Attorneys, the Drug Enforcement Administration, the United States Marshal Service, and the Administrative Office of U.S. Courts, as well as various state and local law enforcement organizations. He is a member of the Department of Justice's Integrated Justice Information Systems Industry Working group.

George Haynal is an assistant deputy minister in the Canadian Department of Foreign Affairs and International Trade, with responsibility for the Americas. Previously he had served for three years as Canadian consul general in New York. Mr. Haynal was also co-chair of the Canada-United States Partnership, an advisory group that reported to Prime Minister Jean Chrètien and President Bill Clinton. In 2001-2002 Mr. Haynal is a fellow of the Weatherhead Center for International Affairs at Harvard University. At Harvard he is carrying out research on North American integration, the impact of disintermediation on the role and functioning of foreign ministries, and international relations management.

Darryl Jenkins is the executive director of George Washington University's Aviation Institute. He is one of the best-known authorities on aviation in Washington, D.C., and is a regular commentator in the national press. He has been involved in the airline travel business for 20 years and has consulted for a number of major airlines. His books include *Financial Distress in the Airline Industry, Failed Partnership*, and *The Handbook of Airline Economics*. Mr. Jenkins served as a member of the Executive Committee of the White House Conference on Aviation safety and Security, at the request of Vice President Al Gore.

Donald P. Moynihan is a research associate at the Alan K. Campbell Public Affairs Institute and a Ph.D. candidate in public administration at the Maxwell School of Citizenship and public Affairs, where he has also received his master's degree in public administration. He received a bachelor of arts from the University of Limerick, Ireland, where he received the Silver Medal, the highest academic achievement in the College of Humanities. Other honors include John K. Kennedy Fellowship, a Syracuse University Fellowship, and a Maxwell Dissertation Fellowship. He has written on various aspects of public management including managing for results, public sector reform in the United States and internationally, human resource management, and public participation in government. His work has appeared in journals such as *Public Administration Review, Review of Public Personnel Administration, Public Performance and Management Review*, and a number of collected volumes. His dissertation deals with the rise of managing for results in U.S. state governments, focusing on the policy area of corrections. His work experience includes time with the World Bank and the Irish civil service system.

Tara O'Toole, MD, MPH, is director of the Johns Hopkins University Center for Civilian Biodefense Studies and a faculty member in the School of Hygiene and Public Health. Dr. O'Toole is a board-certified internist and occupational medicine physician with clinical experience in academic settings and community health centers. From 1993 to 1997, she served as assistant secretary of energy for Environment Safety and Health and was principal advisor to the secretary of energy on matters pertaining to protecting the environment and worker and public health from DOE operations. From 1989 to 1993, Dr. O'Toole was a senior analyst at the Congressional Office of Technology Assessment where she directed and participated in studies of health impacts on workers and the public due to environmental pollution resulting from nuclear weapons production, among other projects. She is a member of the Defense Science Board summer panel on biodefense technologies and the Maryland Department of Health and Mental Hygiene steering group on public health response to WMD events, among other advisory and consultative positions related to bioterrorism preparedness.

Alasdair Roberts is an associate professor in the Maxwell School of Citizenship and Public Affairs at Syracuse University. He is also director of the Campbell Public Affairs Institute. A native of Pembroke, Canada, Professor Roberts received a JD from the University of Toronto Faculty of Law in 1984, a master's degree in public policy from the Kennedy School of Government in 1986, and a PhD in Public Policy in 1993. From 1990 to 2001, Professor Roberts taught in the School of Policy Studies at Queen's University, Canada. He has also held visiting appointments at Georgetown University's Graduate Public Policy Institute and at the University of Southern California's Washington Public Affairs Center. He was a fellow at the Woodrow Wilson International Center for Scholars in 1999-2000 and an individual program fellow of the Open Society Institute, New York, in 2000-2001. Professor Roberts is a visiting fellow at the School of Policy Studies at Queen's University, a member of the Canadian Treasury board Secretariat's Academic Advisory Council, and a member of the editorial boards of Public Administration Review and Public Management Review.

Michael A. Wermuth, is a senior policy analyst with the RAND Corporation and is the RAND project director for work in connection with the Advisory Panel to Assess Domestic Response Capabilities for Terrorism Involving Weapons of Mass Destruction, chaired by Governor Jim Gilmore of Virginia. Before joining RAND, Mr. Wermuth served as deputy assistant secretary of defense for Drug Enforcement Policy; principal deputy assistant attorney general for Legislative Affairs; and chief counsel and legislative director for Senator Jeremiah Denton. Mr. Wermuth's service on active duty and in the U.S. Army Reserve spanned more than 30 years. In 1996, he was mobilized and deployed to the Balkans for Operation Joint Endeavor, serving as Chief of Staff/Chief of Operations of Task Force 21, a major subordinate command of U.S. Army Europe (Forward). He has received the Secretary of Defense Award for Outstanding Public Service and numerous military awards and decorations.